D1475027

FISH WATCHING

IN

HAWAII

by

Russell B. Carpenter
and
Blyth C. Carpenter

Natural World Press
San Mateo, California
1981

Published by Natural World Press
Suite 246, 251 Baldwin Avenue
San Mateo, California 94401

All rights reserved. Copyright 1981 by Natural World Press
under the International Union for the protection of literary
and artistic works (Berne). Published simultaneously in the
United States and Canada by Natural World Press.

Library of Congress Catalog Card Number: 80-85003

First Edition

Carpenter, Russell B., 1943-
    Fish watching in Hawaii.
    Bibliography: p.
    Includes index.
    1. Fishes--Hawaii--Identification. 2. Coral reef fauna--
Hawaii-Identification. 3. Fishes--Behavior. I. Carpen-
ter, Blyth C., 1942-II. Title.
QL636.5.H3C37   597.09969   80-85003
ISBN 0-939560-01-1   AACR2
ISBN 0-939560-00-3 (pbk.)

Table of Contents

To Barbara,
Our Remarkable Friend

All photographs in this book, except the back cover, are by Chris Newbert. The photograph on the back cover is by Philip Carpenter.

All other illustrations in this book are by Rod MacPherson.

Foreword

The Hawaiian Islands, like the fabled Galapagos which so affected Charles Darwin that he conceived the idea that living forms change and evolve by natural selection, are a textbook of life forms, both above and below water. The Hawaiian Archipelago, unlike the stark and uninviting Galapagos, has been inhabitated for several centuries by Polynesian descendants and other arrivals who had sacred reverence for the sea and the abundant bounty which it contains. In spite of their lack of modern scientific sampling equipment and SCUBA diving gear, the ancient Hawaiians had an understanding of the biology of each particular species, and this knowledge imparted a reverence for each fish and invertebrate form such that its harvest was managed to allow its ongoing abundance. *Kapus* were established and enforced to protect the fecund forms during their breeding periods, and death came to those humans who violated them. Now, with the advent of uncontrolled fishing and a population many times what the land will support, the aquatic life of the islands is reduced in number and in size, but fortunately what remains is at least a cornucopia for the mind rather than the body.

This visual feast is manifested in the behavior and coloration of the reef denizens which the Hawaiians now wisely protect. The major contemporary industry of the islands is tourism. The Hawaiian Islands are, without peer, the ultimate travel bargain for mainland Americans or tourists from the west. No Japanese or American tourist can visit the islands without exposure to the variety and diversity of fish life that pervades every aspect of the scenery: as tourists to the hotels, to the culture centers and museums, to the Waikiki Aquarium and Sealife Park, or more intimately, as seen through a diver's or snorkler's facemask. A number of pedantic ichthyological texts are available which enumerate the species, their relationships and their differences, but until now, none have translated such scientificese into the language of the amateur fishwatcher.

This volume is the first to attempt and clearly achieve such a lofty goal. This well researched but easily readable study has digested an enormous library of taxonomic, behavioral, and ecological literature and has come up with eight chapters of delectable stories of fish territoriality, symbiosis, table manners and sexual mores, as well as an illustrated guide to the primary characters that one would see at Hanauma Bay while snorking or off Moku Manu on a 20 fathom plunge. The superb artistry of Rod MacPherson transcends the limitations of photography by accentuating the important postural and color characteristics necessary for the identification of each common species.

The ancient Hawaiians worshipped *Kuulakai*, the god of fishes and fishermen, and his wife *Hinapukuia*, for their ichthyological contributions to the life of the islands. As a modern-day student of Hawaiian fishlife, I would like to dedicate a special *koa* shrine to Russell and Blyth Carpenter, who have brought to the layman a readable, fascinating and enjoyable guide for Fish Watching in Hawaii.

Dr. John E. McCosker
Director, Steinhart Aquarium
San Francisco

Introduction

This book is written for people who enjoy the seashore and have a sense of curiosity and wonder about the natural world. Although the material in the book can best be appreciated and explored by those who take up snorkeling or scuba diving, our aim is to convey a sense of the drama, complexity and humor of the underwater world that will appeal to anyone with an interest in nature.

Snorkeling or diving on a good reef is a three-dimensional excursion into a world gone wild with color and motion. The reef can produce almost more visual complexity than the eyes and brain can absorb. There is something addictive about floating quietly along the reef, doing nothing more complicated than watching the kaleidoscopic patterns of light, coral and other marine life.

That is how our own interest in reef watching began, and the visual satisfactions are still a major reason why swimming along the reef is for us always a fresh experience. But, over time, we have noticed our interests shifting direction. We first moved from a sight-seeing phase to an identification phase. Motivated by our innate curiosity, we acquired all of the books on Hawaiian fishes we could find and began to learn the names of the common species. We still refer to these books frequently and take pride in seeing and identifying new fishes. We have noticed that practically everyone we dive and snorkel with has developed a similar curiosity about identification; we suspect that fish watching is evolving into as fine an art as bird watching did decades ago.

The most satisfying aspect of reef watching occurred for us when we became interested in the behavior of reef fishes. As civilized a sport as fish-identification is, all kinds of basic questions remain unanswered. How does the human observer sort out the intense activity on a reef? Is the reef really as peaceful as it looks, or is it suffused with subtle tensions and drama? Why are many reef fishes so brilliantly colored and, conversely, why are some of them, to the human eye, apparently dull or mis-shapen? What makes a damselfish only six inches long willing to attack a human being? What do reef fishes eat, and what is their sex life like?

Perhaps these questions are best summed up by a statement attributed to William Beebe: "The *isness* of things is well worth studying; but it is their *whyness* that makes life worth living." When we use the phrase "fish watching" in this book, we mean it in this sense.

There is no better place on earth than a reef to study the behavior of wild creatures. Coral reefs are enormously productive, producing a flood of basic nutrients that support the visible reef animals. They are accessible to human observers since, fortunately, the vertical zone most tropical corals live in is almost identical to the diving range of a scuba diver. A coral reef supports a stunning diversity of species within a limited space, a diversity that cannot be matched by any other living space, whether on land or in the water.

Hawaii's marine life is in a much more natural state than its land-based life. Except for several areas of Oahu, the sea life surrounding the Hawaiian Islands comprises the same species and lives in the same places as when the Polynesians first settled the islands. In contrast, the terrestrial environment has been greatly changed by man. Native life forms have been displaced by agriculture and cities, but the more important problems have been caused by man's introduction of non-native animals and plants. Many new animals and plants have replaced their native competitors and in some cases have caused their extinction.

The first chapter of this book, "Beginnings," deals with the general character of the Hawaiian Islands and the inshore reef areas. It briefly discusses the various types of reef fishes and their earliest origins. The chapter concludes with the story of how native Hawaiians caught and conserved marine life and how the fishes influenced their diet and culture. The second chapter, "A Feast for the Eyes," describes the color patterns so characterisitic of reef fishes and investigates some past and present scientific explanations for their prominent coloration.

"Territories," Chapter III, points out examples of territorial behavior among Hawaiian fishes and investigates the purposes of territories. The fourth chapter, "Help," deals with the wide variety of fascinating defense mechanisms used by the reef fishes. And the fifth chapter, "Strange Bedfellows," covers several well-known cases of symbiotic or cooperative behavior.

In Chapter VI, "Making a Living," the fascinating array of feeding methods used by Hawaiian reef fishes is discussed. Chapter VII, "Sex," describes the different approaches to reproduction found among reef fishes, and some intriguing new research on the sex life of wrasses, parrotfishes and angelfishes. Chapter VIII, "Fishes, Fishes Everywhere," presents what might be the most scientifically important aspect of reef life. The chapter explores the issue of diversity — why and how have such an enormous number of diverse life forms evolved to occupy such small living spaces? Chapter IX, entitled "Cast of Characters," contains descriptions of the most common reef fishes in Hawaii, along with color illustrations of each of them.

Scholarly research on the behavior of the reef fishes only began in earnest some fifteen or twenty years ago. The field is in an exciting and growing time, with fresh contributions to knowledge being made constantly. As Davis and Birdsong have said:

> We will soon (if it is not already underway) witness production of a devoted school of sea-invading fish watchers, exploring the great biological frontier of ocean habitats with the remaining myriad problems in behavior, color, habit, habitat interrelationships among members of faunal communities, which have just recently been catalogued.

This book would not have been possible without the scientific work of Randall, Reese, Losey, Hobson and others, many of whose names appear in the *References* section of this book. We are grateful to Dr. John McCosker, Carl Roessler, Chris Newbert, Norma Fifer, Karl and Jill Wallin, and Dr. Leighton Taylor for reviewing and commenting on the manuscript. Dr. Robert Lea provided first-class technical editing. And we thank our friend and colleague Daniel Gotshall for his advice and support.

Chapter I

Beginnings

"Nature never did betray
the heart that loved her."

William Wordsworth (1770-1850)
Lines Composed a Few Miles Above Tintern Abbey

The Setting

To most of us, Hawaii means the familiar group of seven principal islands, including Hawaii, Maui, Lanai, Molokai, Oahu,
Kauai and Niihau. In fact, these are only the southeastern-most
islands in a long, narrow line of islands running more than 1,500
miles to the northwest. The northwestern islands are now
scarcely more than rocks, but they were formed from the same
volcanic activity that created the seven main islands and were
once much larger. The Hawaiian Islands are among the most
isolated in the world, located 2,000 miles from California, 3,400
miles from Japan and 850 miles from the nearest point in the
Society and Tuamoto Island groups. As we will see later, this
physical isolation has encouraged the evolution of a number of
fishes unique to Hawaii and makes Hawaii an ideal place to
observe the process of evolution.

Hawaii is situated in the zone of the northeast trade winds,
and the surface currents generally go from east to west. Although
the average water temperature during the summer is close to
80°, winter surface temperatures can drop to 75°. These relatively cold winter temperatures limit the variety and abundance
of corals, sponges and other invertebrates living in Hawaiian
waters. It is also the reason why a wet suit is almost always a
welcome addition in Hawaii and a virtual necessity for the scuba
diver.

The seven principal islands are in reality enormous moun-
tains, far larger in their bulk and height than any mountain in
North or South America. They begin on the ocean floor which is
itself from 12,000 to 18,000 feet below sea level, and, in the cases
of Muana Loa and Muana Kea, rise to more than 13,000 feet
above sea level. Their slopes tend to be very steep where they
meet the sea, and correspondingly the reef habitats around the
islands are narrow.

Other tropical islands have significantly larger reefs, because over long periods of time waves have eroded the shores
into flat areas known as *benches*, which have in turn served as
foundations for coral reefs. But in the case of the Hawaiian
Islands, the land masses have repeatedly emerged and subsided,
making it impossible for benches to be formed and major reefs

to be built up. The result is that today the coral reef habitat is not dominant in Hawaii and may constitute less than half of all of Hawaii's shallow water areas.

Coral

Most coral grows best in quiet, well-lighted, relatively warm water. In very protected areas, such as Hanauma Bay on Oahu, coral is able to develop profusely only 10 or 15 feet below the surface. In most parts of Hawaii the wave action is too strong at this depth, and 25 to 35 feet is required to escape the surge.

An interesting symbiotic, or cooperative, relationship exists between corals and algae. Although we will say much more about symbiotic relationships in Chapter V, this particular case of symbiosis is fundamental to the entire reef habitat. The algae live within the coral's skeletal structure; nothing about their appearance would otherwise suggest any connection between their life processes and those of coral. In fact, both algae and coral create a number of by-products which are used in the life processes of the other. The algae's by-products allow the coral to form its skeletal structure at a greatly accelerated rate. If the algae are deprived of light, they can no longer sustain photosynthesis and die. In turn, the coral, deprived of its crucial nutrients, secretes its calcium skeleton at only 1/10 its normal rate.

The critical role of algae partially explains why some corals have such a difficult time establishing themselves in the surge zone. The continuous energy released by waves stirs up sediments which in turn block the sun. Only in the relatively quiet water of the sub-surge zone, which allows adequate light penetration, are these corals and their associated algae able to receive enough light for vigorous growth. They are also, of course, protected from the constant abrasion occurring in ocean surge. Some of the best coral colonies in Hawaii are found along the Kona coast, since it is relatively protected from the trade wind seas and winter storm swells. Coral can cover as much as 20%

of the bottom even in the shallower water along the Kona coast, while in waters of 30 to 70 feet, coral cover can be as high as 70%.

The coral reefs around Oahu have suffered to various degrees from water pollution, and in one case the damage became disastrous. Some of the best coral reefs were formerly in Kaneohe Bay, on the windward coast of Oahu. In the early 1960's, dredging, bad land management and excessive sewage produced large amounts of sediment and nutrients in the bay, allowing a bubble algae to take over the coral reef environment. The damage has been especially severe in the middle and south parts of the bay, and reestablishment of the reef environment will probably take decades once environmental conditions are corrected.

Coral Reef Fishes

The coral reef habitat supports an astonishingly abundant and diverse community of fishes. The most common coral reef fishes in Hawaii are butterflies, surgeons, wrasses, parrotfishes, squirrelfishes, goatfishes and moray eels. Although some species tend to favor either the surge or sub-surge zones, many of them can be found in both zones during various times of the day and night. It is not unusual, for example, for the scuba diver to scour the reef at 80 or 90 feet and then see the same species of fishes during a casual snorkel in shallow water 20 feet from shore.

Most Hawaiian reef fishes, and indeed most fishes in the world, belong to a group with the scientific name of "Teleostei." These are the modern ray-finned fishes, and there are about 20,000 species of them. They are the most diverse group of bony creatures in the world, and they occupy almost every aquatic living space.

The ray-finned fishes have a number of advantages over more ancient forms of marine life. Ancient fishes were armored with a dense or rigid skin and had massive and heavy skeletons. The ray-finned fishes lost their external armor and developed a light but strong skeleton. This advanced framework led to the development of another improvement in fish design — the swim bladder. In ancient fishes, the swim bladder was merely an organ functioning much like an internal air tank that could be used as a lung. In modern fishes, this organ has evolved into a buoyancy compensating device, allowing the fish to keep its buoyancy nearly neutral. Since the modern fish skeleton is so light, the buoyancy compensator can be small and compact, generally no larger than 1/12 of the entire volume of the fish.

Another advantage is the one that is easiest to see in a reef habitat and is fascinating in its own right. In the more primitive fishes, such as sharks and rays, fins are relatively fixed and inflexible. But in the modern fish each spine in a fin is moved by its own set of muscles, so that the entire fin becomes supple and flexible. Flexible fins may sound like a humble asset, but in fact they have given modern fishes great maneuverability and corresponding advantages in feeding and defense.

On the average, ray-finned fishes are small, much smaller than the sharks and rays. Their small size allows them to take shelter in many underwater habitats and reduces the amount of food they need. And finally, the modern fishes have clever jaws, more flexible than the ancient versions, and capable of plucking, sipping and snapping food from unlikely places.

Modern fishes have evolved body shapes and attributes to fit the special problems and opportunities on a reef. Many ray-finned fishes have very soft and supple fins, and accordingly are known as "soft-rayed" fishes. They generally live in the mid-water habitats, and the few soft-rayed fishes that do live near reefs tend to hover near the reef, rather than being in contact with it. Many reef specialists have developed spiny fins — primarily for defense in the confined reef environment — and thick scales or skin that can cope with coral's rough surface. Additionally, reef fishes have flexible, specialized mouths, enabling them to feed on the many forms of prey in the reef environment. Finally, reef fishes have rearranged their fins to fit more easily into holes, cracks and crevices. Their pectoral fins, which are immediately behind their gills, have become vertical rather than horizontal, and their pelvic fins have moved forward from the abdominal region to a position nearly as far forward as the pectoral fins.

Origin of Hawaiian Fishes

Hawaiian reef fishes belong to a fauna known as the Indo-West Pacific shore fauna. There are four tropical fish faunas in the world (the Indo-West Pacific, the Eastern Pacific, the Western Atlantic and the Eastern Atlantic), and the Indo-West Pacific fauna is the most diverse. It is the largest faunal area in the world, extending halfway around the world from the Red Sea and the eastern coast of Africa, eastward across the entire tropical Indian Ocean to the western Pacific Ocean. The easterly boundary line for the Indo-West Pacific fauna is along a line from Hawaii to the Tuamotu Archipelago. While there are fishes unique to each part of the Indo-West Pacific, a remarkable number of fishes are found throughout the entire region.

Given the fact that adult coral reef fishes average about 6 inches in length and are not long-distance swimmers by any stretch of the imagination, it is incredible that these small creatures made their way to and occupied a major portion of the earth. According to the most commonly held theory, many of the fishes (or their ancestors) that now live in Hawaii first evolved in the east Indian Ocean near the Malay Peninsula and southern Philippines. This area still has by far the largest number of species of coral reef fishes and is located "upstream" of major ocean currents sweeping to the east.

Some fish larvae are "pelagic" in their nature, meaning that they drift in the open ocean for a fixed period of their early development. Pelagic larvae are being constantly "broadcast" from upstream locations and move hundreds and even thousands of miles until they either die or chance upon a shoreline with a suitable environment. The offspring from these immigrants then begin to disperse their own larvae, and over a countless number of years the Indo-West Pacific coral reef fishes have island-hopped in an easterly and northerly direction.

The theory seems to be proved by the fact that the fishes originally in the east Indian region which had habits and life cycles most appropriate for travel are also the fishes that are now found in distant destinations, such as Hawaii. While the variety of species in Hawaiian waters may be sparse by Indo-West Pacific standards, the variety is large nevertheless. It boggles the imagination to think of the ancestors of all those species making their way across the vast Pacific and arriving at the most isolated islands in the world.

Interestingly, the ocean between the Indo-Pacific and the west coast of the Americas has proved to be too difficult for most fishes to cross. About twenty to thirty Indo-West Pacific fishes have been found along the shorelines of Mexico, Central and South America, but almost none have made it the other way.

Endemic Fishes

About 34% of the Hawaiian reef fishes are endemic, that is, they are found nowhere else in the world. This is an unusually high rate of endemism and has probably been caused by the extreme isolation of the Hawaiian Island group, which gave Hawaiian fishes an unusual opportunity to evolve into new and unique species. A surprising number of the most familiar and common Hawaiian reef fishes are endemic, including the saddleback wrasse, uhu, manini and brown moray. In a few cases, such as the lizardfishes and the cardinalfishes, both the "parent" form of the fish and the endemic form that evolved in Hawaii are currently found in Hawaiian waters. Scientists speculate that the parent form re-entered the Hawaiian region after the original parent had disappeared by evolving into the Hawaiian endemic version.

Some of the changes demonstrated by Hawaiian endemics can be explained as adaptations to colder water temperatures, but most of them seem to have no obvious advantage and might simply be random accidents in the evolutionary process.

Introduction of Fishes

Oddly, in spite of the productivity of the Hawaiian reef habitat, and the great number of species, few of the traditional tropical food fishes are found here. Even though the early Hawaiians were able to fit Hawaiian reef fishes into their diets, to the modern taste most of them are very bony, terrible tasting, or both. Many efforts have been made to introduce new food fishes to Hawaiian waters, especially groupers and snappers found in other parts of the Indo-West Pacific region. Although these efforts have often failed, three transplants have become established in Hawaiian waters. The most successful appears to be a handsome yellow snapper with blue stripes, imported from the Marquesas Islands and known by the Tahitian name of "taape."

Coral Reef Fishes and the Native Hawaiians

The story of the uses of marine life by native Hawaiians gives a fascinating perspective to Hawaiian fish watching. When the first Polynesians arrived in Hawaii, there were practically no food resources available on the land. Birds, bats and edible ferns were about the only food the land could provide, and human life would have been sparse indeed on that kind of diet. Fortunately, the Polynesians already had a culture which emphasized fishing, and they were quickly able to make use of marine foods. By the time Captain Cook discovered the Hawaiian Islands, the natives had developed eight different methods of catching fish. These included collecting by hand, poisoning, spearing, trapping with baskets, nets, fish hooks and lines, and aquaculture. Some of their fishing methods were truly sophisticated. For example, the Hawaiians used four different kinds of nets, including gill nets, seine nets, bag nets and combinations of seine and bag nets. They were able to catch tuna by trolling with lures and to catch bottom-dwelling fishes with hook-and-line at depths up to 1,200 feet.

Fish ponds were perhaps the best example of the early Hawaiians' ingenuity. The ponds were constructed by building stone walls in shallow-water areas of the sea with a number of openings in the walls to allow the water to circulate freely. A mesh made out of wooden poles was placed in the openings to prevent large fish from escaping. It was possible for small fishes to enter the pond through the barriers, but if they remained in the ponds for too long, they grew too large to escape. The ponds constituted an early form of aquaculture, since the fish were fed and husbanded over long periods of time. This book was written on the banks of an ancient fish pond on the Kona coast, no longer used for raising fish, but an excellent place for ducks, small boys and writing books.

Native Hawaiians had an elaborate system of names for fishes, and many of those names are still used. For example, the convict tang is still commonly known as the *manini*, the wahoo as *ono*, and, of course, the dorado or dolphinfish as *mahi mahi*. Some Hawaiian names for fishes are very long and because of the few consonants in the Hawaiian language, genuine tongue twisters. Our favorite is the name for a trigger fish — *humuhumunukunukuapua'a*.

Fishing was an honored profession in ancient Hawaii, and fishing practices were passed down from generation to generation under a surprisingly formal tutorial system. Apparently, the Hawaiians were sophisticated not only in their knowledge of fishing methods, but also in techniques of conservation. When the Hawaiians discovered especially good fishing holes, for example, the fish were fed with sweet potatoes, pumpkins and other vegetables, and harvested on a carefully planned and disciplined basis.

The most interesting aspect of Hawaiian conservation is the use of *kapus*, used by the ruling classes to establish and enforce fishing seasons, so that fishing was prohibited during spawning times. Kapus distinguished between fishes that needed protection and those that did not. Furthermore, kapus were arranged so that they did not overlap excessively, providing a continuous chance to make a living from the sea. Summer was thought to be the time when fishes were most abundant, and kapus were relaxed on almost all inshore fishing. During the winter, deep-sea fishing became lawful, while the season for most inshore fishes closed. Throughout the kapu period, the chief examined the condition of both fish and plant stocks and lifted a kapu only when he felt that the stocks had adequately replenished themselves.

The first fish caught after the lifting of a kapu were reserved for the gods and offered on an alter to the fish god. Next, the best fish were allocated to the chief and his household and to various other members of the ruling class. According to Margaret Titcomb's fine book, *Native Use of Fish in Hawaii*:

> Division was made according to need, rather than as reward or payment for a share in the work of fishing. Thus, all were cared for. Anyone assisting in any way had a right to share. Anyone who came up to the pile of fish and took some, if it were only a child, was not deprived of what he took, even if he had no right to it.

The ancient Hawaiians must have had rugged throats and different taste buds from our own. They took delight in swallowing fish whole — fins, scales, viscera and all. In fact, the Hawaiians believed that removal of the viscera ruined the taste of fish, unless the viscera had been removed to make some powerful condiments. One sobering recipe for viscera condiment called for all of the visceral organs, except the gall bladder, to be seasoned with chili peppers and green seaweed and then to "ripen" for several days. Ripen was, we think, a polite word for advanced deterioration.

Apparently, even Hawaiians felt that certain fish were too strongly flavored. But they developed an ingenious and fail-safe method for rendering a smelly fish more appealing. According to Margaret Titcomb, this was the procedure:

To remove the odor from such fish as the palani, kala or
puwalu, which are good to eat but have a rank odor, lay the
fish across the palms of both hands with the head resting
in the left hand and the tail in the right. Inhale over the fish
from left to right, and expel the breath violently. Turn the
fish over and repeat.

Native Hawaiians had interesting attitudes toward sharks.
While they may have eaten the flesh of several harmless sharks,
man-eaters were subject to a kapu. Indeed, man-eating sharks
were thought to be gods who protected their patrons. Each
region along the Hawaiian coast had its own patron shark, and
one of the local residents served as a keeper, responsible for the
care, worship and well-being of the patron. Serving as patron
shark must have been a pleasant line of work, since the shark's
physical duties were minimal, and the local residents fed him
regularly with such delicacies as pigs and birds.

Chapter II

A Feast for the Eyes

"All orators are dumb
when beauty pleadeth."

William Shakespeare (1564-1616)
The Rape of Lucrece

Nature's Palette

In comparison to more tropical reefs, Hawaiian reefs may seem, at first, drab and colorless. The average seawater temperature in Hawaii is too cold to support the dramatic corals and colorful sponges that are profuse on warmer reefs. Nature seems to have made up the difference, however, with the abundance and color of Hawaiian reef fishes. Butterflyfishes, in particular, have a diversity and boldness of coloration which is hard to match anywhere.

In a typical single-tank scuba dive, one can sometimes see as many as twelve species of butterflyfishes, and most are beautifully colored and patterned. Our own favorite is the oval butterfly, whose contrasting colors and stripes, bold from some vantage points and subtle from others, almost defy description. Another special treat for Hawaiian reef-watchers is the schools of raccoon butterflyfishes that often gather in considerable numbers and create a panorama of yellow, black and white woven in ever-changing patterns. Ornate butterflies are always impressive, especially if seen in shallow water and bright sunshine or under the light of a strobe. The six orange bars across the body of the ornate butterfly can sometimes glow with almost fluorescent intensity. And although there is nothing unusual about the colors and patterns of a long-nosed butterfly, his profile, with impossibly prominent proboscis, is unforgettable.

There are relatively few species of angelfish in Hawaii. Although two of them, the black-banded angel and the flame angel, are handsomely colored and patterned, both are rather rare. A third species, the Potter's angel, is so abundant that it almost becomes commonplace and easy to overlook. To the casual swimmer, the Potter's angel looks rather dull brown, but in reality it is brilliantly colored with yellow, gold and blue hues. This species is also blessed with an interesting sex life, which will be investigated in Chapter VII.

A number of the wrasses are brilliantly colored and patterned. The ornate wrasse is the most complex, with a remarkable pattern of red, blue, yellow, orange, black and green spots and stripes. The yellow-tail wrasse is also distinctive, both in its juvenile and adult stages. As a juvenile, this wrasse is an intense red, with several large white spots. As it matures into an adult it undergoes a complete change of color scheme, ending up with a yellow tail, red fins and a body speckled with blue spots. The cleaner wrasse, about which much more will be said in Chapter V, brilliantly combines iridescent blues and yellows and sometimes seem to almost pulse with color completely out of proportion to its small size.

Parrotfishes are closely related to the wrasses, and some of them are nearly as brilliantly colored, although not as complexly patterned. We will discuss in Chapter VII how individual wrasses and parrotfishes can change their sex and colors. This ability makes identification of many wrasses and parrotfishes difficult and, for many years, caused much confusion in the scientific community. Until fairly recently many of the color-changed wrasses and parrotfishes were thought to be separate species. Research revealed the error, and the number of species has now been substantially reduced.

Most of the surgeonfishes are subtly colored. The principal exception is the yellow tang, with the purest and boldest yellow of any of the reef fishes. Other surgeons are known primarily for a few brilliant patches of colors, such as the red-shoulder tang and the achilles tang. Our own favorite is the naso tang which, in addition to a distinctive body shape, has fascinating patterns of gray, orange, yellow, white and black.

The Moorish idol is impressive by any standard. This most famous of Hawaiian fishes combines a bizarre but somehow graceful body shape with bold and striking patterns of white, yellow and black. Although the Moorish idol resembles butterflyfishes in some aspects and surgeonfishes in others, it is in fact the only species of its own family.

Triggerfishes have clumsy body shapes but with bright body patterns in many species. The lagoon humu, for example, looks as if it were created by a mad artist who brushed streaks of paint and globs of color every which way. The Picasso triggerfish is another common Hawaiian species, and although he is more rationally patterned than the lagoon humu, he is no artistic slouch. Filefishes, puffers, boxfishes and cowfishes are closely related to the triggerfishes and more subtly patterned. Several of them, though, such as the speckled boxfish and the fan-tail filefish are beautifully patterned and well worth the face-to-face examination that these tiny fish require.

Many reef fishes are able to change their colors at will. Squirrelfishes, for example, can change their color from an intense red to orange, and, as described later in this chapter, surgeonfishes use instantaneous color changes as part of their social behavior. But none of the reef fishes can match the octopus (a mollusk, not a fish) who, during periods of stress, can be a living imitation of a flashing neon sign. Not only can the octopus adopt colors which blend perfectly with his surroundings, he can also pucker his skin into all kinds of disguising textures.

Another common color change among Hawaiian reef fishes occurs at night, when many fishes adopt wholly different colors and patterns. The raccoon butterfly, for example, changes from its brilliant daytime yellow into a dull brown. Teardrop butterflyfishes similarly lose their brilliant yellow coloration with their distinctive teardrops standing out boldly against a drab background.

The Mystery of Poster Coloration

Some color phenomena have clear explanations; perhaps the easiest to understand is color as camouflage. Many reef creatures use color and color patterns in a variety of ways to enhance either their defenses or their success as predators, and we will give these fascinating topics a close look in Chapters IV and VI. But for most of the colorful reef fishes there is not such an easy explanation. Their colors and patterns seem almost outlandish. Why has the evolutionary scheme favored reef creatures painted in peacock hues?

This question has preoccupied scientists for decades. Fishes are among the few animals that can see colors, which would strongly suggest that the so-called "poster coloration" of reef fishes must have a purpose. In the early 1900's a popular idea was that poster coloration, which looks so conspicuous when observed in isolation, in fact provides a kind of concealment in the cluttered and confusing setting of a coral reef. While this point of view is encountered occasionally today, it is hard to believe that the theory would ever have developed if the scientists at that time had had scuba gear. While it is true that the background of a coral reef is a jumbled and confused place, it is also true that the intense colors of coral reef fishes stand out distinctly nevertheless.

The question of poster coloration, and perhaps the whole matter of reef fish watching, was brought into public prominence when Konrad Lorenz published his book *On Aggression* in 1963. Lorenz's book examines aggression in broad terms, focusing primarily on the meaning and containment of aggression among humans. Lorenz does make extensive use, however, of information and analogies from the natural world. The book was primarily motivated by Lorenz's experiences scuba diving in the Caribbean and was deeply influenced by the life patterns among fishes he observed. Lorenz posed the central question this way:

> The loud colors of coral fish call loudly for explanation. What species-preserving function could have caused the evolution? I bought the most colorful fishes I could find and, for a comparison, a few less colorful and even some really drab species. Then I made an unexpected discovery: In the case of most of the really flamboyant 'poster'-color fish, it is quite impossible to keep more than one individual of a species in a small aquarium.

Lorenz recognized that on the actual reef most conflicts that are not predatory in their nature are not fatal in the result. The conflicts he observed in his first aquarium generally were

fatal, so he built a much larger aquarium, holding more than two
tons of water. His observations confirmed his belief that fishes
are more aggressive toward their own kind than toward others.
He then concluded that the poster-colored fishes were most territorial and needed their colors to signal their intent to defend
their territories against members of their own species.

Lorenz went on to a persuasive and eloquent discussion
of the specialized ecological niches found on a coral reef. He
pointed out that a coral reef provides a tremendous number of
specialized feeding opportunities for coral reef fishes, ranging
from plankton to crustaceans, to the coral polyps themselves
and so on. Lorenz recognized that these specialized feeding
opportunities cause the evolutionary process to favor specialized
fishes which have adapted to feeding on specific kinds of prey
and specific parts of the reef. Lorenz argued that the greatest
threat to any particular specialist is not the general fish population but other members of his own kind feeding on the same prey.
A species, to survive, must space all of its members over the reef
so that each has an adequate feeding territory to support himself.

Lorenz then related his observations on ecological niches
to his aquarium studies of poster-colored fishes. He concluded
that the purpose of poster coloration in reef fishes is to stimulate
aggressive reactions among fishes of the same species. By this
method Lorenz believed that fishes of the same species keep
themselves adequately spaced out on the reef so that each has
its own food supply and can survive.

Lorenz's book led to a storm of reaction among scholars,
basically supportive in its nature but often critical of the details.
For example, many scientists have pointed out that some of the
dullest colored reef fishes are the most aggressively protective
of their territories. This observation is especially true of certain
damselfishes, some species of which will defend their territories
much more vigorously than any of the other reef fishes, even
though they are often dull and small in size. In Hawaiian waters,
the most casual snorkler will often see damsels protecting their

territories furiously, sometimes against human invaders. Another weakness in Lorenz's argument is that some coral reef fishes are very specialized in their feeding habits but not provided with the bright colors Lorenz thought essential for dividing up the food supply. Still another obvious flaw in Lorenz's hypothesis was pointed out by Paul Erlich, the well-known population biologist. He and several other scholars studied the behavior of butterfly-fishes on Australia's Great Barrier Reef and found very little aggressive behavior among these fishes, notwithstanding the brilliant coloration of many of them.

Lorenz believed that poster-colored fishes are, at all times during the daylight hours, sufficiently colored to send their signals and do not need to change their colors further. In a study of tropical surgeonfishes, George Barlow made some fascinating observations about coloration, all inconsistent with Lorenz's theory. For example, Barlow found that a surgeonfish which is usually black develops a brilliant blue face when chasing other fishes. When angry the abundant and aggressive lavender tang acquires a pale center, with a dark margin around its head and body. Barlow pointed out that the most notable color changes occur with the naso tang — its forehead and pectoral fins become brilliant yellow during a fight, and at times its entire body becomes blue.

One group of observers believes that poster coloration is designed to enable members of the same species to recognize each other readily and thus to avoid cross-breeding among closely related species in a given family. For example, although the many species of Hawaiian butterflyfishes are closely related to each other, many of them seem to be specifically adapted for feeding in a particular ecological niche, that is, upon a particular kind of prey in a well-defined part of the reef. If cross-breeding occurred, these high levels of specialization, which are a distinct advantage in the reef environment, could be dissipated. According to this school of thought, poster coloration is designed to reduce the chances of cross-breeding and to keep the species specialized.

This theory too has some weaknesses. Many species, especially among the butterflies, have remarkably similar colors and patterns, and it is hard to see how the subtle differences in coloration could serve as identification signals. In addition, a number of brightly colored fishes seem to be "generalists" in their feeding habits.

We feel that poster coloration probably has a number of purposes. In certain cases bright colors could allow members of the same species to maintain their physical space on a reef and to recognize each other during breeding. In other reef fishes, the bright colors may have an exactly opposite purpose from that assumed by Lorenz. That is, many brightly-colored fishes, such as some of the butterflies and the Moorish idol, are not territorial, often gathering into sizable and amiable groups. Perhaps the function of poster coloration in these cases is to help members of the same species gather together rather than to repel each other. In other cases, poster coloration may be a danger signal. Most coral reef fishes have flattened body shapes and are armored with spines. They would make a prickly and difficult meal for predators, and one purpose of their bright colors may be to advertise this unpleasant fact.

We will discuss in Chapter IV other aspects of poster coloration with definite defensive purposes. Almost all butterflyfishes, for example, have a black stripe running through the eye which may help disguise the eyes from predators whose preference is to attack the head first. Correspondingly, a number of butterflyfishes seem to have large "false eyes" on their sides, which may either frighten predators away, or confuse their attack. Finally, poster coloration may help reef fishes defend themselves with "flash coloration." This school of thought believes that with flattened body shapes and bright colors, reef fishes are able to display a broad and bright image to a predator and then, when attacked, completely change their appearances by turning either head-on or tail-on. Viewed from either of these perspectives, many reef fishes are so narrow that they seem almost to disappear. Presumably, this almost instantaneous change in appearance would confuse the predator.

Coloration, then, is both a pleasure to the viewer and something of a mystery. The interest shown in the topic by scientists and lay persons alike and the recent flowering of theories mean that poster coloration will remain a lively topic for a long time.

Chapter III

Territories

"Quae est domestica sede incundior?"
(What is more agreeable than one's home?)

Marcus Tullius Cicero (106-43 B.C.)
Ad Familiares

The Variety of Territorial Behavior

Chapter II hinted at a powerful and pervasive aspect of reef life by pointing out that some reef fishes seem to have a home range, which they defend vigorously. We found that the most aggressive territorial behavior seems to occur among members of the same species, and one of the poster coloration theories we investigated was the possibility that bright colors are used as a means to elicit territorial aggression among fishes of the same kind.

In fact, territorial behavior is much more elaborate and interesting than the theories of poster coloration first suggest. Recent research has shown that there is a great variety of territorial behavior on the coral reef.

The best way to see territorial behavior in Hawaiian waters is to get to know the damselfishes. Although most of these fishes seem drab and insignificant, they turn out to have some of the most interesting behavioral patterns among all of the reef creatures. There are fundamentally two classes of damsels — those that feed on plankton and hover several feet above the rock and coral and those that feed on tiny prey on the surface of the reef itself, living close to the bottom. The most territorial of the damsels are those that are bottom-dwelling.

The underlying causes for territorial behavior are easy to understand. Reef fishes depend absolutely on the reef for food and protection from predators. The number of suitable living spaces on any given reef is finite and since reef fishes are so prolific, competition for living space is intense. By staking out a home range, learning its topography down to the last detail, and defending it vigorously, a territorial fish takes out a kind of insurance policy for himself that wandering fishes cannot have.

During the early days of reef fish research it was thought that almost all territorial aggression was directed against members of the same species. More recently, scientists have shown that territorial aggression can be directed against any and all fishes that violate territorial boundaries. The yellow-eyed damsel, for example, was found to have distinct territories and to attack all fishes that crossed the boundaries, whether they were damsels or not. Other damselfish seem to have more flexible boundaries, and the size of the territory and the frequency of attacks seem to be influenced by the degree to which various other species feed on the same food. Damsel territories can also be influenced by seasons and are generally defended with special vigor during the breeding season.

Territorial behavior among other reef fishes definitely occurs but is more complex and less predictable. Surgeonfishes show practically every variety of behavior, including permanent territories, temporary grazing territories or schooling. Parrotfishes and wrasses generally seem non-territorial in their behavior, except that parrotfishes often use well-defined pathways as they move from one grazing spot to another.

A detailed study of Indo-Pacific butterflyfishes by Ernst Reese revealed a number of interesting facts about their territorial and social behavior, particularly relevant to Hawaii since butterflies are such a conspicuous part of reef life. Reese focused on pair bonding which is unique to the butterfly species. Most species of butterflies apparently form lifetime male-female pairs. Some of these pairs occupy well-defined territories while others maintain less well-defined home ranges and still others wander from place to place. Reese did observe a certain amount of agression among members of the same species, but as a whole the aggressive behavior was less than expected. Aggression also occurred when members of different species violated territorial boundaries, but it was generally limited to those other butterflyfishes that fed on the same food sources as the territory holders. Reese felt that the territory holders learn to recognize neighboring butterflies by their appearances, and this fact, coupled with the "advertisement" from their bright color patterns (discussed in Chapter II), helps to keep actual outbreaks of aggression to a minimum.

The inherent aggressive tendencies of territorial fishes, especially against their own kind, could make life very difficult for juvenile fishes. There are, apparently, adaptations to keep juvenile fishes alive until they have reached maturity and can hold their own in the territorial struggle. Most strikingly, the juvenile offspring of brightly colored coral fishes often have completely different color schemes from their parents. These juveniles can invade the territories of their elders in complete safety, while an invasion from the mature form of the same fish would provoke a furious reaction. In other cases, juvenile fishes occupy different living spaces from the adults; the larval stages of many fishes float freely in the ocean, often far from the home reef. Somewhat more advanced juvenile fishes take up residence in shallow water and tide pools and migrate to the reef only when they are large enough to stake out and defend territories of their own.

How the Non-Territorial Fishes Cope

If the entire reef were divided into territories, and if the holders were perfectly successful in defending their territories, there would be no opportunity for non-territorial fishes to make a living. In this case, as in so many others explored by this book, we see how the evolutionary system devises a means for survival. Non-territorial fishes often gather into schools and use the tactical advantages of cooperative behavior to defeat the territory holder. Although schooling also is an important defense mechanism against predators (as we will discuss in Chapter IV), it is possible that in a reef environment the most important function of schooling is to enable a school of fishes to overwhelm a territory defender.

Since damselfishes depend so strongly on their territories, they are also the principal victims of schooling fishes. One study focused on parrotfishes and found that those parrotfishes that elected to join schools were much more successful at feeding than solitary individuals. The solitary parrotfish was attacked and driven off by the resident damselfish almost every time he invaded a territorial boundary while the same parrotfishes feeding in a school could swamp and defeat the damselfish's defense.

Damselfish might have an acute reason to defend their territories against parrotfishes. Parrotfishes enjoy munching on the same rocks and corals to which damselfishes attach their eggs, causing parrotfishes to become the ultimate neighborhood pest from the damsels' point of view.

The manini, one of the most familiar fishes on Hawaiian reefs, was the subject of a similar study. Almost all of the surgeonfishes have "scalpels" at the base of their caudal fin which give them a formidable means of defense against predators. The scalpels on a manini are, however, comparatively small, and the fish is at a considerable disadvantage. Manini are famous for their large swirling schools, and it is tempting to think that the primary purpose of these schools is to create protection from predators that the lightly armed manini would not otherwise have. A more important purpose may be to permit the manini to swamp defenses of their principal feeding competitor, the very aggressive lavender tang. The study showed that schooling reduced the number of attacks against manini by lavender tangs by at least 30%.

Chapter IV

Help!

"Lighten our darkness,
we beseech thee, O'Lord;
and by thy great mercy
defend us from all perils
and dangers of this night."

The Book of Common Prayer (1789)

Using Color for Defense

Every reef fish is, of course, another reef fish's potential meal. A few reef animals are so well-equipped with weapons, such as the moray eel, or thoroughly disguised, such as the frogfish, that their lines of defense are obvious. But most reef fishes seem peaceable and bucolic, and one wonders how they survive from day to day. The truth is that even these fishes have been provided with surprising and crafty defenses.

Color patterns are one common method of defense. Many predators depend on their eyesight to a considerable degree, and scientists have demonstrated that fishes are misled by the same kinds of optical illusions as human beings.

The simplest kind of color pattern defense is called countershading. A countershaded fish has a dark upper body and a light belly. A predator looking at a prey fish from above is fooled by countershading since the fish's back blends in with the dark background created by the absorbtion of sunlight in the lower water. A predator looking up might also be fooled because the fish's light underbody blends with the sunlight streaming down from the surface. The combination of light and dark in countershading also makes fishes difficult to see from the side.

Countershading would seem to be most effective for fishes that live in the well-lit regions of the ocean close to the surface, and indeed most open ocean fishes feeding near the surface are countershaded. Simple countershading is much less common on the reef.

Another kind of color defense is called disruptive coloration and consists of the same kinds of irregular stripes, spots and patterns used to disguise warships and airplanes. These markings do not mimic the fish's background in any exact way, but somehow the total effect is to confuse the eye and break up the outline of the fish. Tropical groupers are probably the best example of disruptive coloration, but few live in Hawaiian waters. Another example, more common in Hawaii, is the freckled hawkfish. The hawkfish's body patterns are certainly not an exact duplication of the surrounding reef and rock patterns, but the fish, which is able to lie perfectly still, can be amazingly difficult to see. Just about the time a snorkler or scuba diver thinks he is developing a sharp eye, an unseen hawkfish will make a dash for cover six inches from his mask.

Yet another form of color defense, known as deflective markings, was first mentioned in Chapter II. Many butterfly-fishes, wrasses, and damselfishes have one or more eye spots on their bodies or fins, which generally look like a bull's-eye surrounded by a ring of different color. The fish's true eyes are generally masked with bands of colored pigment. Scientists have observed that predators often attack the eyes of their prey first. They theorize that the eye spot tricks the predator into charging for the wrong eye, allowing the victim to make a quick escape, usually in apparent reverse.

Some fishes are able to duplicate either their background, or other fishes or plants, with amazing accuracy. Perhaps the best known example is the seahorse, which looks more like a small plant than a fish. But the true geniuses are found among the predators. Lizardfishes, scorpionfishes and angelfishes look so much like lumps of rock or coral, complete with encrusting vegetation, that often the observer has to stare intensely at the object before he can tell it is a fish. One of the more sobering sights on a reef is that of a harmless looking "rock" exploding out of the sand and swallowing a careless fish with one gulp of its large and very toothy jaws.

For a final look at the use of color as a defense, we turn to the squirrelfishes and bigeyes. Although many of these fishes can change their color at will, their predominant coloration is a deep red. Red would normally seem about as useful a camouflage color as international orange, and it is doubtful that the red color of squirrelfishes evolved primarily for defensive purposes. But red is not the liability it seems because it is one of the first colors to be filtered out of the light spectrum by seawater. On the deeper portions of the reef, the red component of sunlight has almost disappeared, leaving these fishes a nondescript gray. (Gray, in fact, is a more elusive color than black, since a black fish can be seen by its silhouette, while a gray fish disappears into the turbidity.) Furthermore, most of these fishes spend the day hidden in caves, feeding only at night. Even in strong moonlight the red portion of the light spectrum would be almost gone, and the fishes would be difficult to see.

Schooling

The ocean is full of small, peaceable fishes which seem to have no defenses at all. Given the speed, power and ferocious appetites of many predatory fishes, one wonders how defenseless fishes survive. By forming a swirling, turning aggregation, small fishes present such a multitude of opportunities that the predator cannot concentrate on a single victim. More often, the predator will charge the school, but it will charge blindly and without results. Although this aspect of schooling, known as the "confusion effect," may be the most important defensive use of schooling, it is also possible that a tightly packed school may resemble a large fish and frighten predators. Furthermore, from a mathematical point of view, it would appear that packing prey fishes into a single group would reduce the probability of encounters with predator fishes. And, since predators can only consume a given quantity of prey fishes before they become satiated, it follows that with fewer encounters a greater number of prey fishes will survive.

For reasons that are not entirely clear, schooling becomes a less effective defense during morning and evening twilight periods. In other tropical waters, predation increases dramatically at dawn and sunset, a phenomenon well-known to fisherman the world around. Edmund Hobson argues that the period of maximum predation in other tropical waters is actually a relatively quiet period in Hawaii. The nocturnal fishes have not yet left their daytime hiding places, and the daytime fishes have moved toward the bottom of the reef and reduced their activities.

Hobson believes that this difference between twilight conditions in Hawaii and other tropical areas seems to have two causes. First, many of the small bait fishes that live in the inshore areas of other tropical locations, and which form dramatically large and complex schools, are not found in Hawaii. Secondly, as we found in Chapter I, Hawaiian reefs lack many of the major predatory fishes that are common on other tropical reefs. Except for the taape introduced from the Marquesas Islands, which is still not truly abundant in Hawaii, there are virtually no snappers and groupers on Hawaiian reefs, and sharks and barracudas are relatively scarce.

Another defense tactic used by small fishes is known as pilot behavior. For example, one of the Hawaiian jacks, in his juvenile stage, spends much of his time as a pilot of larger predator fishes, especially sharks. The young jacks swim directly in front of the shark's jaws but seem to be safe either because they are out of sight or are too small to interest him. Hitching a ride with a shark is, of course, a crafty way to stay safe from other predators. In addition, the juvenile jacks are pushed along by the shark's bow wave and, with little effort, can cover long distances.

Hiding

A number of other reef fishes bury themselves in sand when threatened. The pearlscale razorfish is especially clever at digging. It is not unusual for the fish watcher to see this rather chunky fish make a death-defying plunge straight toward the sand and disappear. Many other wrasses dig into the sand as a defense. They have narrow and streamlined heads apparently designed to facilitate their burrowing.

Garden eels are another fish that use sand as their castle. These eels live in large clusters in the deep, sandy fringe of the reef and spend their days with their heads and upper bodies protruding from their burrows, swaying back and forth in the current. Garden eels can retract their bodies into their burrows in a flash. There are often several jacks patrolling this part of the reef, and they periodically make furious dashes at the garden eels. Generally, they get nothing but exercise.

For all of their apparent fragility, butterfly and angelfishes have effective defense tactics. Their narrow, laterally compressed bodies fit readily into the cracks and crevices of a rock or coral reef. When threatened, a butterfly or angelfish can make a quick disappearance into the nearest crack. If they are cornered without cover, they raise their dorsal and anal spines, presenting the prospect of a prickly and painful meal. These fishes can also swim backwards and dodge over-anxious predators.

In contrast, triggerfishes are slow moving and non-maneuverable. Although they have a leathery skin and strong jaws and teeth, they seem to have been cheated of most defense mechanisms. They do have one defensive adaptation which seems to work well enough to keep the species going. The front spine of the dorsal fin of a triggerfish is long and strong. Furthermore, there is an internal mechanism in the fish which can lock the spine in an upright position. If the triggerfish is severely threatened, it will head for a crevice in the reef and wedge itself there by erecting and locking the spine.

Parrotfish have an interesting means of defense during the night. Many of them rest in a quiet crevice or crack in the reef and secrete a thick mucus cocoon around their bodies. The cocoon is transparent and soft, and it could not inhibit any serious attack. Scientists believe that the principal purpose of the cocoon may be to cut off the smell of a parrotfish from predators who hunt at night principally by smell, particularly moray eels. Apart from schooling, parrotfishes do not seem to have any defense mechanisms during the day.

The Improbable Puffers

The most bizarre, but probably the most famous, of defense mechanisms among Hawaiian reef fishes occurs in pufferfishes. Seen in their free-swimming form, puffers look like jokes. They are flaccid, slow-moving and docile, and one wonders how they make it from day to day. A pufferfish under attack, though, will immediately gulp in mouthfuls of water and puff itself up to three times its original size. Some of them can also erect a multitude of strong and sharp spines. Even a dim-witted predator must realize that the puffer is too large to fit in his mouth or throat, and even if he could fit, too prickly to eat.

Chris Newbert, an experienced diver and photographer from Hawaii, takes a different point of view. He points out that pufferfishes chased by divers inflate only *after* they have been captured. If their reaction to natural predators is the same, then inflation would occur too late to be an effective open-water defense. Newbert believes that the real purpose is to enable pufferfishes to wedge themselves in caves and crevices.

Pufferfishes have a second line of defense. Many of them are among the most poisonous fishes in the world, because their liver, gonads, intestine and skin contain a nerve poison that produces rapid death, even among humans. Scientists are not sure whether the poison is also effective against the puffer's normal predators, and, if it is, whether the predators have learned so. The Japanese convert the pufferfish's poisonous qualities into a kind of culinary thrill. One of the classic prized dishes of Japan is called *fugu*, which consists of a pufferfish sliced into thin strips, arranged into artistic patterns and eaten raw. The pufferfish is prepared by well-trained and specially licensed cooks, with great care.

Poisonous and Venomous Fishes

A cousin of pufferfishes, the boxfish, is a delight to the human observer but a mysterious creature. His almost rigid body is heavily armored with bone. About all he can do to move from place to place is flap his pectoral fins, which are not impressive either. But boxfishes show little fear of either swimmers or predators. This habit makes them easy to observe; one would think it would also make them easy to eat. Their armor must help in their defense, but it is also known that some of the boxfishes secrete a poisonous toxin from their skin, which may be the key to their survival. The quickest way to demonstrate the poisonous secretions from a boxfish is to place an upset one in an aquarium. All the other fishes die promptly.

There are venomous fishes in Hawaiian waters that deserve respect — the scorpionfish, and the closely related lionfish. Hawaii has a number of species of scorpionfishes, all of which sit quietly on the bottom waiting for unwary fishes to pass by. They are extremely well camouflaged, and it is all too easy to touch or brush one by mistake. Scorpionfishes are covered with sharp spines that have been modified to serve as injection needles for poison glands. The most venomous fish in the world is a scorpionfish known as the stonefish, but fortunately he is not found in Hawaiian waters. Not all Hawaiian scorpionfishes are venomous, but they should all be treated with care.

The lionfish, although a nasty customer, is genuinely spectacular. It combines bold color patterns with luxurious spines and fins and poison as potent as any of the other Hawaiian scorpionfishes. The lionfish seems to be fearless, perhaps because it understands the power of its defenses. Although most of the scorpionfishes seem to simply wait until a meal swims by, the lionfish is apparently capable of herding small fishes into a crack by spreading its fins and spines wide and cutting off escape.

Surgeonfishes have an obvious and effective means of defense. Most of them have a knife-like spine located on both sides of the body, immediately in front of the tail. These spines are generally hinged and lie along the body in a sheath. When the surgeon is aroused or frightened, it will erect the spines and flash its body from side to side. The spines can inflict deep gashes; predators seem to take this threat seriously, and humans are advised to do so without qualification. Surgeonfishes will not go out of their way to threaten any creature larger than themselves, and it is possible that their principal use of the spines is to defend their territory or interests against others of the same species.

Chapter V

Strange Bedfellows

"The only reward of virtue is virtue; the only way to have a friend is to be one."

Ralph Waldo Emerson (1803-1882)
Essays: First Series. Self-Reliance.

Common Forms of Cooperation

Is the coral reef a dog-eat-dog kind of place, with all of its inhabitants intent on eating each other, or, at best, maintaining an uneasy tolerance? The answer is that although most reef fishes spend much of their time eating, avoiding being eaten, and reproducing, there are distinct and important examples of cooperation.

Perhaps the most obvious form of cooperation is schooling, which we have discussed in Chapter IV. Insofar as schooling is intended to confuse and defeat predators, or to defeat the holders of territories, it is a clear example of cooperative behavior among fishes. And, as we will see in Chapter VII, schooling is critically important to the sex life of many reef fishes.

There may be a more generalized cooperative purpose in schooling. Food supplies for any given species of fish are usually concentrated in a few places. A school allows a group of fish to function as a kind of super-fish, with more eyes and brains, and a greater ability to scan the environment, than any single fish could ever have. Once any member of the school finds a supply of food his feeding behavior attracts the rest. Finally, schooling may literally function as a kind of "school." Fishes seem to learn more quickly and develop a better memory than isolated fishes of the same species. Most schools consist of fishes of about the same size and about the same stage of development, and it is possible that one of the purposes of schooling is to enable these fishes, who share common problems and a common environment, to learn from each others' experiences.

Another important but more subtle example of a cooperative relationship is the one between coral and algae, described in Chapter I. As quiet and unassuming as this example of cooperation is, it is essential to the formation of the entire reef environment.

Cleaning Behavior

The most dramatic and famous example of cooperative behavior on a coral reef is called "cleaning symbiosis." Just like their terrestrial counterparts, fishes suffer from tiny parasites that live on their skin. This small misfortune leads to an intriguing drama among seemingly unrelated fishes. Throughout the tropical reefs of the world, including the reefs of Hawaii, certain small fishes have become specialized as cleaners and operate "cleaning stations" with efficiency and with respect for complex rules and procedures. At first impression, the cleaning phenomenon seems to be an almost perfect example of a symbiotic relationship. The parasites constitute a food supply for the cleaner fishes, and the client fish gets rids of parasites which can cause it considerable irritation and even death.

Most of these parasites are crustaceans which live either on the surface of the skin or between the fish's gill arches. The parasites probably produce an itch in a fish, and many fishes attempt to scratch themselves against rock or coral, or even against other fishes.

The client fishes apparently know where each cleaning station is located and sometimes patiently form a line. Many juvenile fishes, such as young butterflies, angels, wrasses and damsels, clean adult fishes on a regular basis but seem to lose their cleaning habit as they mature. Shrimps also serve as cleaners, apparently throughout their lifetimes. But the truly professional cleaners are two strikingly similar groups of fishes: in the Atlantic, the professionals are the cleaner gobies, while in the Indo-Pacific they are the cleaner wrasses. The cleaner wrasse in Hawaii is a brilliant little fish with bold striped colors of yellow, black and violet. The cleaner gobies from the Atlantic are similarly striped, and, interestingly, so are a number of the juvenile fishes that serve as cleaners during their youth. There is at least a possibility that their strongly striped body patterns help establish the cleaning relationship with client fishes.

During the cleaning process, the cleaner swims close to the client fish, inspects his body, and pecks away the parasites on his skin. He may enter the client's mouth and gill cavities. The cleaner wrasse applying his trade shows no fear, even if the client is a moray eel, who from the perspective of most small fishes must be repugnant indeed. Apparently, the cleaner's clients include practically every other reef fish. Scientists have been fascinated by the cleaner's ability to establish effective communications with such a wide variety of partners.

The communication signals between the cleaner and client have been studied carefully, and a "body language" has been identified. The most obvious signals occur when the client first "poses" in front of the cleaner. The client may shake and shimmy, change coloration, roll over, or do both head and tail stands. The cleaner fish's inspection of the client may also be a formalized means of communicating. Still another signal may occur if the client fish fails to stay still, at which point the cleaner will jab it violently with its wide open mouth. It is also common to see cleaner fishes engaged in a kind of "dance" which may serve either to attract a client in the first place, or to reduce the tendency of an aggressive looking client to attack the cleaner. Finally, client fishes may jerk their bodies as a means of signaling the cleaner that the session has come to an end.

There is even a possibility that these signals are effective on a worldwide scale. In an experiment at the Steinhart Aquarium in San Francisco, Caribbean groupers, which are normally cleaned by Caribbean cleaner gobies, were placed in an aquarium with the same Pacific cleaner wrasse we see in Hawaii. The Pacific wrasse is larger and moves differently from its Caribbean counterpart but, as we have mentioned, it is patterned similarly. The groupers were initially confused by the wrasses, but after a remarkably short time allowed the wrasses all of the normal cleaning latitudes.

In another experiment, all the cleaners were removed from two small reefs. Within several weeks, virtually every fish had abandoned the reef, and the few that remained were developing parasitic white spots on their bodies. The same experiment was tried in Hawaiian waters, with considerably different results. After the cleaner wrasses had been removed, fishes that normally served as part-time cleaners substantially stepped up their cleaning activity. Apparently, there was little migration away from the reef by client fishes, and no evidence that the level of parasitic infestation had increased.

Carl Roessler calls the whole cleaning process a "negotiated truce." He feels that most of the cleaning fishes are considered tasty tidbits by the hosts who are so courteous during the cleaning procedure. In one experiment, he extracted a number of cleaner shrimp from a reef and photographed them in open water. As soon as they were removed from their customary cleaning stations, their former clients swooped by for a quick snack.

There is a final twist in the story. A small fish, known as the saber-toothed blenny, just happens to bear a remarkable resemblance to the cleaner wrasse and is able to imitate his behavior signals. Enter the innocent client. The saber-toothed blenny swims up to the client with the normal reassuring signal and then takes a bite out of his fin and eats it. Apparently, the blenny's act works only with young and naive fishes, and those who are older learn to avoid him.

Cleaning symbiosis is a deeply interesting topic, and scientific research on the cleaning phenomenon is certain to continue. Some recent research, for example, has opened a whole new line of questions. Careful study of the stomach contents of cleaner wrasses has shown that they were eating at least as much of the client fishes themselves, in the form of mucus, scales and bits of skin, as parasites. Scientists are now wondering whether the cleaner wrasse is as beneficial to the client as once assumed and, if not, why the cleaning phenomenon seems to be so strongly imbedded in the behavior of all tropical reef fishes.

Remoras

Another well-known example of cooperative, or at least tolerated, behavior occurs between sharks and remoras. The remora's dorsal fin is highly modified, to form a powerful suction cup that allows it to attach itself to the shark's underside. The cup is shaped in such a way that the faster the shark moves through the water, the more strongly the remora clings to the host. Remoras do not derive any nourishment directly from the shark. They swim about actively whenever the shark is feeding and seem to feed upon plankton and scraps left from the shark's prey. The shark thus provides the remora both with a form of transportation and a meal ticket. Apparently, the remora does not provide any direct benefit to the shark, but it causes him no harm.

Remoras will attach themselves to many different kinds of fishes, even though sharks are their most usual hosts. This habit is used to man's advantage in some parts of the tropics. The natives capture a remora, attach a line to its tail, and return it to the sea. The remora diligently looks for a host, and as soon as it has attached itself to a fish or turtle, the fisherman pulls both of them back to the boat. Romoras, though, are capable of revenge. Karl Wallin, during one of his underwater photography expeditions, unwittingly became a host for a remora which attached himself to Wallin's thigh and enjoyed a free ride for the entire dive.

1. Blue Ulua. An open water predator cruising the reef.

2. Arc-eyed Hawkfish. His characteristic ambush posture.

3. Freckled Hawkfish. Standing his ground.

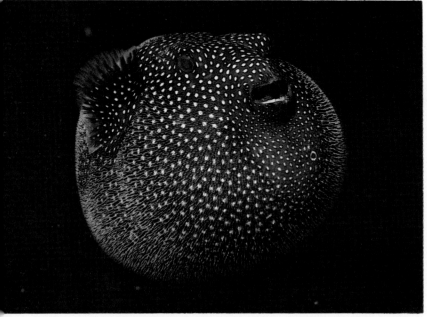

4. Spiny Balloonfish. Showing body inflation as a defense.

5. Hawaiian Lionfish. The most venemous of Hawaiian reef fishes.

6. Moray Eel with Cleaner Wrasse.

7. Saber-toothed Blenny. The imposter.

8. Ugly-faced Scorpionfish. A master of camouflage.

9. Gobie. Another striking case of camouflage.

10. Moray Eel. Things that go bump in the night.

11. Parrotfish. Showing his fused teeth, adapted for feeding on coral.

12. The neighbors discovering unguarded eggs.

13. Trumpetfish. A mouth adapted for vacuuming small prey.

14. Long-nosed Butterfly. Another specialized mouth, for reaching prey in cracks and crevices.

15. Banner Butterflyfish. Schooling behavior.

16. Freckled Hawkfish with an unfortunate Filefish.

Chapter VI

Making a Living

"Third Fisherman: . . . Master, I marvel how the fishes live in the sea."

"First Fisherman: Why, as men do aland; the great ones eat up the little ones."

William Shakespeare (1564-1616)
Pericles

To our way of thinking, feeding habits of reef fishes are one of the more puzzling aspects of fish watching. Fishes seem to divide themselves into two groups. One group seems to be constantly munching away at something, but the prey is too small to see. The other group eats prey large enough to see but seems to spend most of its time waiting around for the opportunity. When the opportunity finally does arise, they engulf their prey in such a flash that the eye and mind can scarcely follow the action. Edmund Hobson has made exhaustive and fascinating studies of the eating habits of Hawaiian fishes and has found that the Hawaiian reef is really three worlds in one. During the periods of daylight, twilight and night, entirely different communities of fishes are active and make their livings in unique ways.

The Daytime Specialists

The daytime tends to be the world of the specialized feeder. During the day, many prey creatures have their defenses at full alert — the sunlight allows them to see their predators and to take refuge in the reef and in other instances to form schools which confuse their predators. Thus, predator fishes have had to evolve a whole array of specialized feeding methods to overcome these defenses. We have observed six different ways to make a living during the daytime — demonstrated by the sippers, pluckers, crunchers, stalkers, ambushers, and bottom feeders.

The least specialized daytime feeders are the sippers. These fish dart around several feet above the reef looking, as far as the naked eye can tell, as if they are doing nothing useful. In fact, the sippers are constantly locating and sipping tiny organisms in the daytime plankton. The largest number of sippers come from the damselfish family, although a significant number of the damsels are bottom feeders and some, like the sergeant major, will eat anything at all. One of the damsels is a perfect example of a sipper. It has a small, upturned mouth suitable for catching minute prey, and its eyes are far forward on its head where they can focus on prey that must intrinsically be extremely difficult to see. This damsel has a streamlined body and deeply encised tail fin, which enable it to swim rapidly. These adaptations may be the key to the damsel's survival, since it is quite exposed to predators as it forages for plankton throughout the reef and needs to be able to make a quick getaway.

Pluckers

The largest number of fishes that make their living during the day fall within the category of pluckers. This group constitutes the great number of fishes — butterflyfishes, wrasses, angels, damsels, and others — that seem to spend their day browsing about the reef and plucking at nothing. In fact, they are locating and eating small organisms, usually invertebrates, that live on the surface and in the cracks of the reef. Many of them are eating the coral polyps themselves.

These prey animals have developed a remarkable array of defenses that the pluckers must cope with. Some of them are poisonous or noxious, others have armor, some have spines, and still others have stinging cells. To overcome these defenses, the plucker fishes have evolved a wide variety of specialized feeding techniques. As we will discuss in greater detail in Chapter VIII, this single fact may be the reason why reef fishes have evolved in such diverse directions, and why the reef is such an interesting place to visit.

Sponges are a good example of a protected prey animal that has stimulated predator specializations. Although they cannot move, and thus are easy to catch, sponges cannot be digested by the systems of most reef fishes. In Hawaii, however, the black-banded angel has evolved a digestive system that can handle sponges and so has the Moorish idol. Other fishes, including the long-nosed butterfly and the threadfin butterfly, have developed equipment for tearing off pieces of larger invertebrates. Both of these fishes have long noses, and it is easy to see how their snouts have become specialized instruments for their feeding habits.

Coral polyps are another difficult food for reef fishes. A few of the most advanced fishes have mastered the art of feeding upon coral, and they include certain of the butterflyfishes, damsels and parrotfishes. The butterflies and damsels take the delicate approach and, by using their small mouths, long noses, and fine teeth, are able to snip off individual polyps. Parrotfishes, on the other hand, use the brute force method, as we will see when we discuss the crunchers.

Surgeonfishes are among the other pluckers and also among the relatively small number of reef fishes which are plant eaters. Plant eating fishes are very thorough, causing coral reefs to be devoid of seagrasses and other marine plants. In an interesting experiment John Randall, of the Bishop Museum in Honolulu, placed an artificial reef in a seagrass bed. The plant eating fishes who lived in the reef quickly ate all of the grass in a well-defined ring around the reef, but they were unable to venture any farther than a safe distance from the reef, which provided their only protection from predators. This band of relatively barren territory around coral reefs seems to be characteristic of tropical seas around the world and has been named the "Randall Zone," although recent evidence suggests that sea urchins may be the primary consumers of plant life in this habitat.

Crunchers

Parrotfishes are lavishly equipped with dentation and are the reef's best known crunchers. The teeth on both jaws are fused to form a parrot-like beak, which enables the parrotfish to bite off sizable chunks of coral with ease. Furthermore, a set of grinding plates located farther back in the fish's mouth grinds the coral into smaller pieces. By the time a parrotfish's digestive system has finished with coral, only fine sand remains, which is defecated by the fish in regular and unmistakable displays. Countless sandy beaches on tropical shores were created in this humble but effective way.

Scientists are not entirely certain about the nutritional objective in the parrotfish's consumption of coral. They believe that he is primarily a plant eater and may therefore be eating coral for its associated algae rather than the coral polyps themselves. The polyps browsed on by butterflies and other small coral eaters are often able to regenerate themselves, while the polyps consumed by parrotfishes are destroyed entirely, and in large number. This apparently clumsy and wasteful feeding habit is, fortunately, more than offset by the coral's ability to grow.

In a way, triggerfishes may be the ultimate crunchers. Triggerfishes make up for their slow, sedentary habits by their ferocious ways of eating. For example, almost no other fishes are able to bother a long-spined sea urchin. But the triggerfish has strong teeth and jaws and eyes set back far in its head. Apparently, the triggerfish can simply charge the sea urchin and bite off its spines, with its eyes safe from the spines' reach. The triggerfish then turns the urchin over on its back and eats its internal organs. There is some evidence that the triggerfish is also able to eject a strong stream of water from its mouth against the sea urchin to blow it over.

Our final examples of crunchers are the balloonfishes, puffers and porcupinefishes. In all of these fishes, the teeth are fused and form either one or two plates in the upper jaw and one or two in the lower jaw. They have very powerful jaws and are able to catch and crush crabs and other powerfully-armed invertebrates. One of the classic amusements for divers is to catch these fishes and to cause them to inflate themselves. In so doing, it is wise to remember that their teeth and jaws are no joke.

Stalkers and Ambushers

Since the reef is a confined place, and because defensive mechanisms work well in daylight, most of the predators who prey on other fishes during the day cannot depend on speed of pursuit. Instead, they have developed wily ways to either stalk or ambush their prey. In Hawaii, the best examples of stalkers are the trumpetfish, cornetfish, needlefish and barracuda. Needlefish and barracuda are relatively infrequently viewed by divers in Hawaii, but based on studies in other tropical areas they are known to drift quietly and slowly into range of a prey fish, and then to engulf the victim with a sudden lunge and inhalation.

This is the same basic method used by the trumpet and cornetfishes, except that they are not strong swimmers, especially compared to the barracuda, and must depend on stealth to an even greater extent. Both of these fishes have tube-like snouts and are able to vacuum in their prey with a single gulp of water. But this method of feeding requires the trumpet and cornetfishes to get close to their prey, and trumpetfishes will often form temporary alliances with larger fishes, such as the parrotfish. As a parrotfish passes by, a trumpetfish will take a position along its back and hold this position relentlessly. The parrotfish, while grazing on the coral, often stirs up small organisms that it does not eat itself. Many smaller fishes know this, and are attracted by the parrotfish's feeding activity. Little do they know that concealed behind the harmless parrotfish is a trumpetfish who can vacuum them down his tubular snout in a flash.

The ambushers consist of four exceedingly lazy groups of fishes: the lizardfishes, scorpionfishes, flounders and hawkfishes. All of these fish are poor swimmers and spend their time waiting patiently in a single place for an unwary victim to swim by. Most of them have enormous mouths and can capture their victims in a single gulp. The ambushers tend to be quite difficult to see, and the human observer underestimates their numbers. In fact, both the scorpionfishes and hawkfishes are very widely distributed in Hawaiian inshore waters. An amusing underwatersport is to approach hawkfishes and scorpionfishes slowly and gently while they remain fixed to their perch, with only their twitching eyes betraying that they are there, and that they know that you are almost there. This game should be practiced with caution in the case of scorpionfishes, since a number of them have venomous spines.

Hobson points out a puzzling aspect of certain hawkfishes, especially the freckled hawkfish. Although we mentioned in Chapter IV that the color patterns of certain hawkfishes may be a good example of disruptive coloration, the freckled hawkfish is much easier to see than most of the other ambushers. Hobson speculates that this ambusher may be one of the few that has evolved visible coloration to attract small fishes. It is possible that as long as just a few ambushers are colorfully patterned, those few could benefit from the curiosity elicited among small prey.

Bottom Feeders

Goatfishes, the marine equivalent of fresh water catfish, are perhaps the best example of bottom feeders. Goatfishes have a large pair of barbels, covered with sensory organs, directly under the chin and use these barbels to probe the sandy bottom where they find their prey. They are resourceful predators and can successfully feed on many prey animals that are protected from less specialized fishes.

Various species of the goatfishes feed during both the day and night, tending to concentrate on crustaceans at night and small fishes during the day. At least one species of goatfish has very long barbels, which it uses not only to locate small fishes but also to drive them into the open. Interestingly, a species of goatfish known as the *weke* has a bright yellow stripe along its body when congregating in schools, which is replaced by a single black spot when the same fish are actively foraging for food.

Various rays are also bottom feeders, and watching them at work can be dramatic. The eagle ray, for example, has teeth which are consolidated into a large grinding plate in each jaw. He feeds along sandy bottoms and eats clams and other invertebrates by digging into the sand with his lower jaw. The wing span of a typical eagle ray is about four feet, and these large swimming surfaces can generate enough power for the eagle ray to plow a furrow across the bottom. All kinds of tiny organisms are stirred up from the sand, to the delight of the band of smaller predatory fishes that generally follows the feeding ray wherever he goes.

Twilight

The reef undergoes great changes during the twilight period, presenting new opportunities for different fishes to make a living. Again, Edmund Hobson has provided many new insights into the reef environment at twilight. The changeover begins about fifteen minutes before sunset, when the smaller damselfishes that feed on plankton several feet above the reef descend toward the reef as the light diminishes. The smallest damselfishes take shelter in the reef first, and many other small fishes, such as the wrasses, begin to move toward cover at the same time.

Meanwhile, however, other species of fishes, even though they are daytime feeders, become especially active at twilight. Some fishes become unusually aggressive in defending their territories. Other fishes, such as certain surgeonfishes, parrotfishes, triggerfishes and filefishes mill around in large mixed schools several feet above the reef, until approximately fifteen minutes after sunset. Still others, including other species of the surgeonfishes, parrotfishes and damselfishes, migrate in large numbers along pathways that seem to remain fixed in the same locations over days or even weeks of time, from their daytime feeding areas to the parts of the reef where they will rest for the night.

At this point, both the small daytime and small nighttime fishes are under cover. The larger daytime fishes are swimming about above the reef, and although they are still in schooling formations, the schools have become less effective against predators. The principal twilight predators in tropical waters are groupers, jacks, and snappers. Although groupers and snappers are relatively scarce on Hawaiian reefs, jacks are well represented. It is at twilight that the power and speed of jacks become impressive and effective, as they pick off various prey fishes with attacks of almost chilling competence.

Even though twilight predation appears to be more pronounced in other tropical reef areas, it is nevertheless a definite and dramatic phenomenon on Hawaiian reefs. The principal victims of twilight attacks appear to be the goatfishes, small members of the jack family, and, in particular, several members of the herring family.

Nocturnal Fishes

By about fifteen minutes after sunset, the activity of the remaining daytime species is markedly reduced, as even the larger daytime fishes begin to settle down into nighttime shelters. Concurrently, the larger nighttime species start to emerge from their own hiding places. All of a sudden, herds of fishes, principally squirrelfishes, emerge from the reef. Most of the squirrelfishes hover above the reef during the nighttime, much as their counterparts, damselfishes, do during the daytime. The bigeyes emerge from their hiding places at about the same time, but they rise high above the reef and swim offshore.

Most nocturnal fishes are far less specialized than those that make a living during the daytime. They feed primarily on plankton, but at night the plankton consists of relatively large crustaceans. Thus, squirrelfishes have larger mouths than dam-selfishes that feed on much smaller plankton during the daytime. Since there is a different threat from predators in the open water during the night, squirrelfishes are heavily armored and less streamlined and consquently less speedy than the plankton-feeding damsels.

Moray eels are the most notorious of nighttime feeders. Most of the daytime fishes rest quietly during the night in the crevices and cracks of the reef, and morays have evolved ex-tremely specialized features to defeat this nighttime defense. They are strong and aggresive fishes whose only enemies are large jacks and sharks.

Morays hunt primarily by smell. Their pectoral and pelvic fins have disappeared, and their skin has become thick, tough and scaleless. The head of a moray eel is elongated and has a very strong and solid skull. All of these adaptations allow the morays to manuever through the crevices of the coral reef. With their strong skulls, they can wedge through small openings and can wiggle out of almost any hole they enter. Most morays have large needle-sharp teeth, making it possible to hold onto relatively large fishes, which are either swallowed whole or broken into several pieces. Like most terrestrial snakes, the moray eel has distensible jaws, throat and stomach and is able to swallow sur-prisingly large prey. One study found that the stomachs of moray eels were usually empty and hypothesized that morays do not need to eat frequently. Since moray eels are abundant on many Hawaiian reefs, it is fortunate for every other reef inhabitant that the moray does not appear to be greedy.

Chapter VII

Sex

"Is sex necessary?"

James Thurber (1894-1961)
Title of book

Basics

Most reef fishes spawn externally, producing enormous numbers of eggs. The eggs are fertilized by the male who swims near the female during spawning and ejects his sperm. The eggs of almost all fishes are less than a quarter inch in diameter, and most marine species of fishes lay eggs that float to the surface and become part of the general plankton. The majority of freshwater fishes produce non-buoyant eggs, and as we will see later in this chapter, a few well-known reef fishes also produce non-buoyant eggs.

Some families of reef fishes bear their young live — the best examples are many of the sharks and rays. All male sharks and rays have specially developed organs called claspers, formed from the inner sides of the pelvic fins, which are used to transmit sperm to the females. The embryos develop within the female a number of different ways, but typically the embryos first live off the nutrients contained in the yoke of the egg and later live from nutrients that are secreted by the female's oviducts.

Since external fertilization is overwhelmingly characteristic of reef fishes, we will concentrate for the remainder of the chapter on different modes of external fertilization. Much is left to chance with this method of reproduction. Even if the male and female perform with precise timing, the ever-present currents in ocean waters mean that the eggs will be exposed to the sperm for only a brief time and that many eggs will not be exposed at all. After fertilization, the risks increase. Most reef fishes demonstrate no parental care and simply abandon their eggs after mating. The eggs rise to the surface and float around helplessly, becoming part of the plankton and a food supply for the many plankton eaters.

The life cycle of the manini gives a good example of how hazardous and complex reproduction can be for a reef fish. Manini lay floating eggs, and a female may release up to 40,000 eggs per spawning. The larvae drift with the plankton for about 2½ months; countless numbers are consumed by plankton predators, and countless others drift away from the Hawaiian Islands. Larvae that have survived their initial rigors move inshore with the tides, generally at night and with a new moon. By this time, they are shaped like a disk, about an inch long, and have a translucent body. Interestingly, they have developed weakly venomous spines, which they lose in later life.

Juvenile manini then move into tidepools where they can be caught from February to October. They grow quickly in the tidepool environment and, when they have reached sufficient size and power, finish their long journey by moving back to the reef and their permanent habitats.

In general, surgeon fishes are known for their habit of "launching" their eggs by swimming in a frantic dash toward the surface and ejecting their eggs into the upper waters. John Randall observed this spawning behavior many years ago; at first he thought that the upward movement was primarily designed to confuse predators. Later he decided that the main function was to help the fish discharge their sperm and eggs. The swimbladder expands during the rapid dash to upper waters, increasing pressure on the gonads. The flexing of the body, as the fishes change direction at the surface and turn downward, may also help to release sperm and eggs and to mix them together. But current research tends to confirm Randall's initial suspicion, because the loss of fertilized eggs to plankton predators is markedly less when eggs are released toward the surface, and the eggs also benefit from the outward currents found in the surface water.

Beleaguered Males

Damselfishes, which are so interesting to observe in other contexts, also have interesting sex lives. First, they are among the minority of reef fishes that have non-floating eggs. Secondly, sergeant majors in particular provide all kinds of fireworks in their sexual habits. In the first step, the male sergeant major establishes a breeding territory, very often in rocky areas adjacent to coral formations. Territories are generally three to eight feet in radius, and the male also selects a specific nesting site within the territory, consisting of a hard smooth surface. The male then cleans the surface of its algae and invertebrates.

At this point, the male has developed some fancy nuptial colors. Armed with his new finery, the male engages in an elaborate mating display. When he spies a female, he swims in loops away from his spawning site toward the female. If the female is interested, she starts to follow the male back to the site. Perversely, the male repeatedly turns and chases the female during the trip back to the nest site, at which point both fishes swim very rapidly in tight circles over the nest site. This "tail on tail" chasing apparently stimulates spawning by the female; the male then fertilizes the eggs and chases the female away.

The male damsel's duties have only begun. He is a fearless and aggressive guardian of the nest and will charge even large fish and swimmers. He fans the eggs with his fins to provide them with oxygen and removes defective eggs. If there is a sufficient number of females near his territory, the male can maintain up to five nests within his territory at various stages of development. It is impossible, of course, to protect all the eggs all the time, and predation is severe. A large number of reef fishes appear to be fond of damsel eggs, and the discovery of an unprotected nest site can produce a literal feeding frenzy. For all of his heroism during the eggs' development, the male damsel has his limits and abandons the tiny damsels as soon as they have hatched.

Damselfish males are not only responsible for the housekeeping aspects of reproduction, they provide a kind of musical accompaniment as well. At a critical point in the courtship routine, the males produce a series of pulsed "chirps." A recent study examined acoustical communication among various Caribbean damselfishes and found that the main purpose of chirping is to allow different closely related species of damselfishes to distinguish each other. The scientists made tape recordings of several species and found that the "song" of each differed minutely but definitely from the others. The recordings were played back to mixed groups of damsels, and in most cases the only species responding was the one whose chirp was being played.

There are several other unemancipated males among the reef species. Cardinalfishes are small, nocturnal and generally red in color. In many aspects, they resemble squirrelfishes and spend their days hidden in similar reef hiding places. A number of cardinalfish species practice oral incubation, meaning that they carry their eggs around in their mouths until they begin hatching. In most species, the male cardinal assumes the incubation responsibility, although in some of the species both the male and female appear to share the duty.

Perhaps the most complete role reversal occurs with pipefishes and seahorses. Hawaii has at least two kinds of seahorses, the most common being the spotted seahorse, and several kinds of pipefishes. The male fishes have brood pouches on their belly and are responsible for the incubation of the eggs. Females have highly specialized oviducts, which are used to transfer their eggs into the brooding pouch of the male. Pipefishes and seahorses seem to engage in a series of embraces, with the male going through various contortions between each embrace, apparently to move the most recently deposited eggs toward the back of his brood pouch. The eggs are fertilized by the male while they are in his pouch and then incubated until they hatch.

As the young fishes grow, the brood pouch swells considerably. Delivery by the male can, in some cases, be a true case of labor. The male contorts, strains and sometimes needs to rub his abdomen on objects to help expel the young. Apparently, the male seahorse gives birth some four to five weeks after mating.

Butterflies and Angels

Hawaiian butterflyfishes generally seem to use a much simpler approach to reproduction. Some species appear to spawn in pairs and others in groups, but in all cases the female butterflies lead the males. As the butterflies swim along the reef, the female tilts her head downward and the male swims up and places his snout on her abdomen. At this point, both fish quiver and release their eggs and sperm.

A recent study uncovered many interesting aspects of reproduction among Potter's angels. The Potter's angel is an attractive little fish but illusive and shy. At courtship time, however, these fishes lose their inhibition and put on quite a display.

The male initiates courtship about an hour before sunset. He swims toward the female with undulating motions, stops above her, and erects and flutters his fins. Maintaining his courtship display, the Potter's angel slowly drifts upward. If the female fails to follow him, he swims back down and starts all over again. When the female has been enticed, the pair head for the tallest coral or rock formation in the area. Spawning always seems to occur about three feet over this formation. The male approaches the female from underneath and presses his snout against the abdomen, apparently using the same signal employed by butterflies. As soon as the eggs and sperm have been released the pair dashes for cover.

Phil Lobel has made several interesting interpretations of the Potters' spawning behavior. He points out that spawning at dusk is a good way to reduce predation on the eggs since, as we pointed out in Chapter VI, many of the daytime plankton eaters are then seeking shelter in the reef. But dusk is also the time when the twilight predators are at work, and it must be a very dangerous time for these angels to have left their shelter. The danger from predators may explain why Potter's angels choose to spawn over the highest reef structure. If they are attacked by a predator, there is at least a chance that they can dash to shelter.

Lobel also found that Potter's angels' spawning was influenced by the phase of the moon. Most of the spawning took place during evenings of the first quarter of the moon. Since this is also the time of the month when the tide is generally ebbing at dusk, the eggs may be benefited because they will be swept out to sea with the outgoing tide. Possibly, the phase of the moon is simply acting as a cue to the species to help both the male and female fishes to be ready to spawn at the same time. It is also possible that if a number of different species are cued by the moon to spawn at the same time, any plankton eaters still active at dusk will quickly be satiated, and a larger number of eggs can escape. Finally, since most larvae are attracted to light, spawning during a full moon may stimulate them to swim toward the surface and away from the reef dwelling plankton eaters.

Lobel's research showed that Potter's angels, along with several other species, tended to reproduce most actively from December until June. During this time of the year, currents in the Hawaiian Islands tend to flow in a northwesterly direction, parallel to the islands themselves. During the period of June to December, the currents shift to the southeast and run perpendicular to the islands. The eggs and larvae of Potter's angels, and most other Hawaiian reef fishes, drift in the open ocean with the plankton for a number of weeks. The purpose of spawning primarily during the winter months may be to maximize the chance that eggs and larvae will drift to other Hawaiian inshore areas, rather than drifting into the open sea.

Remarkable Sex Lives of Wrasses and Parrotfishes

This chapter will close with the story of the reproductive habits of wrasses and parrotfishes, which can only be described as baroque. Scientists have long known that the wrasses and the parrotfishes undergo both sex and color changes during their development, but only recently has the true complexity of their sex lives come to light. Although much of the research was done in the Caribbean, the wrasses and parrotfishes of Hawaii are similar to their Caribbean counterparts, and the general principles from Caribbean research may apply to Hawaii as well.

Wrasses seem to have more variety in their lifestyles, so we will start with them. During the early periods of development the males and females are colored alike and act alike. But the females of some species ultimately are able to change into "supermales," which are larger, more brightly colored and more territorial than the fishes that had been male from birth.

The small true males are known as initial phase males, while the males created by females changing their sex are known as terminal phase males. The interaction between the initial and terminal phase males is strongly influenced by the particular kind of social or mating system a species has adopted. Some species mate in *leks*, which are formed when males congregate at temporary mating sites and defend these small areas against the intrusions of other males. The other form of mating is called the harem system, in which males maintain permanent territories containing a group of females with whom the dominant male mates exclusively.

A final distinction needs to be made to make sense out of the wrasses' sex life. *Pair spawning* occurs when a single male mates with a single female. *Group spawning* takes place when two or more males fertilize the eggs of one female. With this terminology in hand, we can look at the duel mating strategies seen in the wrasses.

One would think that the terminal phase males would have all of the advantages. They are, after all, larger and more colorful than the initial phase males and better able to establish and maintain mating territories. Their very potential for success, however, can also be their downfall. As males of all species know, including humans, it is not easy to manage one female, much less many. In large populations of wrasses, the terminal males struggle constantly to protect their empires. This is especially true in species that use the lek system, since the terminal male holds only temporary spawning territories and is unable to establish and maintain a familiar and constant group of females.

Initial phase males have developed two forms of direct attack on terminal phase mating known as *streaking* and *sneaking*. In sneaking, the initial phase male stealthily enters the territory of a terminal phase male who is busy mating with another female and sneaks a sexual event with one of the females waiting for the terminal phase male to finish. In streaking, the initial phase male has the audacity to join the terminal phase male and the female at the climax of spawning. Initial phase males are most successful in large population groups and/or large reef areas. In both cases, the number of females available, or the amount of territory to be protected, is simply too much for the terminal phase male to cope with. But in areas with smaller populations, or smaller sized reefs, terminal phase males are able to establish effective leks or harems, Faced with these disadvantages, the actual number of initial phase males declinclines.

Even with the odds against them, and reduced in numbers, the initial phase males have some tricks in reserve. Initial phase males are, after all, virtually identical to females, and this improves their chances to penetrate a terminal phase male's territory. Once over the boundary line, there is always the chance of a streak or sneak. Terminal phase males can distinguish between females and initial phase males if they closely examine their vents, but they are often too busy and consequently a little careless.

At the opposite end of the spectrum, when initial phase males are very numerous, there is not even a need to resort to streaking or sneaking. Apparently, a large territorial male is able to defend his territory against about a dozen initial phase males, but a larger group of initial phase males can defeat him. At that point, the initial phase males engage in group spawning with all of the females in the defended territory.

Unfortunately, what was an advantage to the lone initial phase male turns out to be a disadvantage to a gang of them. These males have the same difficulty distinguishing females from their fellow initial phase males that the terminal phase males did. According to the research, about 50% of the time groups of wrasses spawning with each other contained not a single female. The final indignity is that the initial phase males become preoccupied with their efforts to group spawn, and many of them are eaten by predators.

A female wrasse's change of sex into a terminal male can be controlled by her social environment. Thus, for example, in the case of our old friend the cleaner wrasse, social groups consist of a single male and a harem of females. If the males dies, the senior female rapidly changes into a male. Her sex change is something of a race, since there is always a possibility that a neighboring male may incorporate the dead male's harem into his own harem.

The sex life of parrotfishes is essentially parallel to that of the wrasses. Population density seems to be less important in the evolution of mating strategies. In wrasses, the more dense the population, the better chance initial phase males have in succeeding. The correlation is weaker in the case of parrotfishes, probably because they are generally much larger fishes and more dispersed over the reef.

The mating system used by the different species of parrotfishes remains an important factor in the success of initial phase males. Parrotfishes that use the harem system have very few initial males, since the terminal phase male is able to dominate his females in the same ways observed with wrasse harems. On the other hand, parrotfishes using the lek system of mating have many initial phase males. In general, parrotfishes reinforce the notion that a number of sexual types and strategies can coexist within a single species. These actually strengthen that species' ability to survive by providing a flexible means of reproduction to meet the challenges of various habitats.

Chapter VIII

Fishes, Fishes Everywhere

"It is interesting to contemplate an entangled bank,
clothed with many plants of many kinds, with birds
singing on the bushes, with various insects flitting
about, and with worms crawling through the damp earth,
and to reflect that these elaborately constructed
forms, so different from each other, and dependent on
each other in so complex a manner, have all been
produced by laws acting around us."

Charles Robert Darwin (1809-1882)
The Descent of Man

In this chapter we deal briefly with the subject that is creating perhaps the most curiosity and excitement among coral reef watchers. The cloud of fishes on a coral reef is not only a pleasure to the eye, it is a scientific mystery as well. The number of different species on a reef and the small space in which they coexist are difficult to explain by present ecological principles.

As the well-known population biologist Paul Erlich has said, "Perhaps the best general description of the way the reef fish fauna is fitted into the reef is 'crammed.' " For example, during the studies conducted from the artificial habitat called "Tektite" in the Caribbean, researchers found 53 resident species of fishes in a single reef only nine feet in diameter and five feet tall. When the species who visited the reef on a regular basis were added to the population, a total of 75 species made their living in and about that small patch of the sea. Startling population counts have come from studies where the fishes in the small area on a reef were poisoned and then collected. In one case, on the Australian Great Barrier Reef, 150 different species were collected, and in another experiment on the island of Palau, 200 species were found.

Feeding Specialists

Those who carefully read Chapter VI of this book, dealing with the feeding habits of fishes, are probably now offering an answer. As pointed out by Lorenz, Hobson and others, the reef apparently offers a large number of highly specialized feeding opportunities. It is only logical that a large number of specialized predators should have evolved, complete with various mechanisms to prevent them from interbreeding and weakening their feeding specializations.

Living Space

We admit that we have been holding back some information. As powerful and simple as this explanation is, there are now many scientists who are suggesting other ones. For example, the researchers participating in the Tektite program decided that feeding specializations were much less important than specializations intended to cope with the limitations of living space.

They first pointed out that reef fishes seldom show any symptoms of malnutrition or starvation and that their numbers tend to remain stable throughout the year. These researchers felt that if there were a shortage of food, and if fishes required high degrees of specilization to make use of limited food resources, evidence of malnutrition or at least changes in populations would occur. In contrast, they felt that the nooks and crannies of the reef were the assets in short supply, and that the amazing diversity in reef fishes represents various adaptations to allow reef fishes to exploit every conceivable living space.

The Tektite scientists thought most reef fishes had very precise "homesite" requirements. Their evidence suggested that if a particular reef lacked the kind of cracks and crevices that could shelter a specific kind of fish, then that species simply was unable to survive there. Although most fishes actively feeding or foraging on the reef were alert and ready to protect themselves from predators, a homesite was crucial in providing those fishes with equally effective protection while they were resting.

A good example of the living space theory is seen with the saber-toothed blennies. You will recall that the saber-toothed blenny is the dastardly little fish that imitates the cleaner wrasse with a view toward preying on the client fish, rather than on his parasites. The saber-toothed blennies are very demanding in choosing their homesites and are able to use only those holes in the reef that meet their exact dimensions. These rigid requirements for living space severely limit the population of saber-toothed blennies on an individual reef. In an interesting experiment, a researcher provided some supplemental artificial nesting blocks with blenny-sized holes in them and was able to double the population of blennies on the reef being studied.

The Lottery

A completely different point of view is being taken by scientists working in Australia. Their data suggests that most reef fishes are not specialists in their living space or eating habits at all. They feel that while reef fishes may prefer certain broadly defined living spaces on a reef, they are not highly demanding in their living space requirements. In addition, the Australian researchers believe that the majority of reef fishes will take advantage of the opportunity, as it presents itself from time to time, to eat a wide variety of foods.

They look at life on a coral reef as a giant lottery. A fish living in a particular homesite on a reef is there, they think, not because he is able to eat the food there, or because he is able to fit into the nooks and crannies, but simply because he got there first. These coral reef fishes have a high degree of mortality, but at the same time produce an enormous number of eggs that float about freely in the ocean. Just as soon as a living space is made vacant by the death of its occupant, the lottery operates and selects, by chance, one of many available species to reoccupy the space. As explained by Peter Sale:

> Thus, the species of a guild are competing in a lottery for living space in which larvae are tickets and the first arrival at a vacant site wins that site.... Single vacant sites are unpredictably generated and are filled by individual colonists, to be held until those fish also disappear and are replaced by new colonists of their own or of other species. ... Thus, chance successes by one species may not lead to that species progressively usurping all living spaces within habitats of that type from other species in the lottery.

Although the Australian research presents good reasons for how diversity of species could be maintained, once it is established, the studies do not throw much light on why the diversity should have emerged in the first place. The evolutionary need to exploit specialized feeding opportunities, or exploit specialized living spaces, somehow seem to be easier explanations to grasp.

These theories are milestones in our understanding of ecological principles. The coral reefs have given both scientists and lay persons a matchless opportunity to observe the patterns of life firsthand. To our way of thinking, coral reefs are therefore both esthetic and scientific treasures, in Hawaii and everywhere they are found.

Chapter IX

Cast of Characters

"Accuse not Nature, she hath done her part;
do thou but thine."

John Milton (1608-1674)
Paradise Lost, Book VIII

Common names for fishes can be confusing. They often arise by casual local usage, and over time a species can acquire a remarkable hodgepodge of names. Scientific names are precise and consistent, but unintelligible to the non-scientist. We have chosen to use common names in this book, but since our choice of a common name may not be the same as yours, the scientific names included in this Cast of Characters will provide a meeting ground.

Information on the size and distribution of Hawaiian fishes is based primarily on *Fishes of Hawaii* by S. W. Tinker, the most recent and comprehensive scientific book on Hawaiian fishes available at the time of printing.

AHOLEHOLES
Kuhliidae

AHOLEHOLE
Kuhlia sandvicensis

Probably restricted to Hawaiian waters. Can be 12 inches in length. Bright silver body, generally found in schools.

ANGELFISHES
Pomacanthidae

POTTER'S ANGELFISH
Centropyge potteri

Range is limited to Hawaii. A small angel, measuring only 3 or 4 inches in length. Nondescript at a distance, but its brilliant colors come to light with close examination. Orange over the front and upper portions of the body, with a great number of vertical blue and black lines on the center and lower parts of the body.

BLACK-BANDED ANGELFISH
Apolemichthys arcuatus

Known only from Hawaiian waters. About 7 inches in length. Color scheme is simple, but striking. White on the lower body, light brown on the upper body separated by a prominent horizontal black stripe.

BIGEYES
Priacanthidae

BIGEYE
Priacanthus cruentatus

This fish is found in all tropical seas throughout the world. It can be up to 12 inches in length. This fish can readily change its colors, ranging from red to a mottled pattern of silver and red.

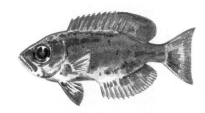

BOXFISHES
Ostraciidae

SPECKLED BOXFISH
Ostracion meleagris camurum

Species ranges from Hawaii to the coast of Africa. This particular subspecies is unique to Hawaii. Around 6 inches in length. A common species, with different coloration and patterns in the males and females. Males are blue, green and brown, with small white spots on the back and a golden band on the head. Females are dark blue with small white spots.

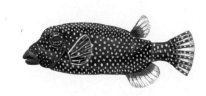

BLUE-SPOTTED COWFISH
Lactoria fornasini

Ranges from Hawaii to the coast of Africa. To 6 inches in length. Most easily identified by its 2 prominent horns on the head, and smaller but distinctive horns at the end of the body. Greenish body with blue spots.

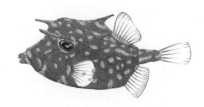

BUTTERFLYFISHES
Chaetodontidae

LONG-NOSED BUTTERFLYFISH
Forcipiger flavissimus

Ranges from Hawaii to the coast of Africa and the Red Sea. Generally 4 to 5 inches long. Body is bright yellow, top of the head is black or brown. It is easily identified by its prominent snout.

FOUR-SPOT BUTTERFLYFISH
Chaetodon quadrimaculatus

Ranges from Hawaii to central Polynesia and southern Japan. Up to 6 inches in length. Top of body is black and marked with distinctive white spots, lower part of body is yellow.

PYRAMID BUTTERFLYFISH
Hemitaurichthys polylepis

Ranges from Hawaii to the East Indies. 5 to 7 inches long. Easily identified by the truncated white pyramid on its side. Upper body is orange, and face is brown.

THREADFIN BUTTERFLYFISH
Chaetodon auriga

Ranges from Hawaii to the Indian Ocean, to the coast of Africa and the Red Sea. One of the larger butterfly species, and reaches 6 to 9 inches in length. Most easily identified at a distance by sets of parallel stripes at right angles to each other. Body is grayish white with yellow upper parts. At close range, the filament extending from the dorsal fin is visible.

BANNER BUTTERFLYFISH
Heniochus diphreutes

Ranges from Hawaii to coast of Africa and the Red Sea. Also known as the poor man's Moorish idol. Can reach 7 inches in length. Body is white, with 2 wide black stripes, and fins are yellow.

ORNATE BUTTERFLYFISH
Chaetodon ornatissimus

Ranges from Hawaii to Arabian Gulf. About 7 inches long. Body is white, marked with 6 parallel and very striking orange stripes. One of the easiest butterflies to identify from a distance.

LINED BUTTERFLYFISH
Chaetodon lineolatus

Ranges from Hawaii across the Indian Ocean to the coast of Africa and the Red Sea. The largest butterfly in Hawaiian waters, reaching a length of 12 inches. Identified by approximately 16 vertical black lines on a white body. Black bands through the eye and below the dorsal fin.

RETICULATED BUTTERFLYFISH
Chaetodon reticulatus

Ranges from Hawaii to Philippines. About 6 inches in length. From a distance, looks dark and nondescript, but close examination shows intricate pattern of gray, yellow and red markings. Black band through the body and fine pattern of light spots on the body.

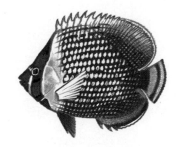

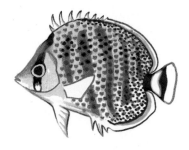

PEBBLED BUTTERFLYFISH
Chaetodon multicinctus
    Known only in Hawaiian waters. A small, brownish butterfly, to 5 inches, best identified by 5 or 6 dark but fairly faint vertical bands on a background of small spots.

LEMON BUTTERFLYFISH
Chaetodon miliaris
    Found only in Hawaii. Another small butterfly with a bright yellow body. Has vertical rows of small dark spots on the side.

BLUESTRIPE BUTTERFLYFISH
Chaetodon fremblii
    Known only from Hawaiian waters. About 5 inches in length. Body is yellow and has 8 or 9 horizontal blue stripes.

RACCOON BUTTERFLYFISH
Chaetodon lunula
    Ranges from Hawaii to the coast of Africa. Reaches 6 or 7 inches in length and seems larger because of its robust body. Has various shades of yellow and 3 black bands. Best identified by its resemblance to a raccoon.

TEARDROP BUTTERFLYFISH
Chaetodon unimaculatus

Ranges from Hawaii to the coast of Africa. 5 to 7 inches in length. Colored with shades of yellow and easily identified by a teardrop shaped black spot on the upper center of the body.

OVAL BUTTERFLYFISH
Chaetodon trifasciatus

Ranges from Hawaii to the coast of Africa. About 6 inches in length. A strikingly beautiful butterfly, with a golden body and 18 or more parallel stripes. The fins are beautifully marked by black and red bands.

CARDINALFISHES
Apogonidae

UPAPALU
Apogon menesemus

Found primarily in Hawaii. Up to 9 inches in length. Body is muted pink and silver; most easily identified by black bars on all fins.

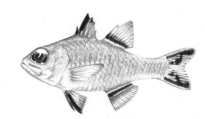

DAMSELFISHES
Pomacentridae

ONE SPOT DAMSELFISH
Dascyllus albisella

Found only in Hawaiian waters. Up to 5 inches in length. A black body, with a virtually round shape when viewed from side. Most easily identified by its prominent white spot on its upper body.

SERGEANT MAJOR
Abudefduf abdominalis

Ranges from Hawaii to central Polynesia. Up to 9 inches in length. A light green body which is boldly marked by 5 vertical black stripes.

KUPIPI
Abudefduf sordidus

Ranges from Hawaii to the coast of Africa and the Red Sea. About 5 inches long. The body is brownish gray and quite drab, but the fish is remarkably pugnacious and an active member of the coral reef community.

YELLOW-EYED DAMSELFISH
Pomacentrus jenkinsi

Ranges throughout the central Pacific Ocean. Up to 5 inches in length. Another drab brownish damsel, but can be identified by its yellow eye. It is also a pugnacious and active fish.

FILEFISHES
Monacanthidae

FAN-TAIL FILEFISH
Pervagor spilosoma

Found only in Hawaii. Can reach 5 inches in length. Most readily identified by its many black spots. A beautiful fish upon closer examination, with yellow body and orange tail.

BROWN FILEFISH
Cantherines sandwichiensis

Also found only in Hawaii. To about 5 inches in length. The most common filefish in Hawaii, with blue and yellow lines on the head and white spots on a brown body.

SCRIBBLED FILEFISH
Aluterus scriptus

World-wide distribution, including tropical seas of the Atlantic, Pacific and Indian Oceans. A very large filefish, capable of reaching 40 inches in length. Easy to recognize, not only by its size and shape, but also by the distinctive brown spots and blue lines on an olive colored body.

GOATFISHES
Mullidae

KUMU
Parupeneus porphyreus

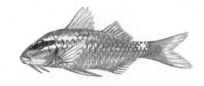

Ranges from Hawaii to Polynesia. Up to 16 inches in length. Body is mottled red and white with a dark line running along the side of the body. Has several white spots on its back.

MOANO
Parupeneus multifasciatus

Ranges from Hawaii and possibly across the Indian Ocean. Can reach 12 inches in length. Also has a mottled appearance, with black, red, yellow and white markings. Has a number of black markings along the back.

WEKE
Mulloidichthys samoensis
Ranges from Hawaii across the Indian Ocean to the coast of Africa and the Red Sea. Up to 18 inches long. Has a generally white body with a yellow line from the head to the tail.

HAWKFISHES
Cirrhitidae

FRECKLED HAWKFISH
Paracirrhites fosteri
Found from Hawaii to the coast of Africa and the Red Sea. Can reach 9 inches in length. Upper part of body is brown, lower is white. Easy to distinguish by its many black spots on front of body.

JACKS
Carangidae

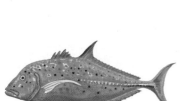
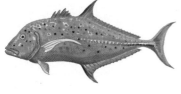

BLUE ULUA
Caranx melampygus
From Mexico to the coast of Africa. Up to 36 inches long. An unmistakable fish, with a blue-green upper body and silver sides. Adults acquire dark spots over entire body.

LIZARDFISHES
Synodontidae

VARIEGATED LIZARDFISH
Synodus variegatus
Ranges from Hawaii to the coast of Africa and the Red Sea. Up to 14 inches long. Brown body with about 9 bands on back and sides. Most easily identified by its short snout, large and upturned mouth, and many teeth.

MOORISH IDOL
Zanclidae

MOORISH IDOL
Zanclus canescens

Ranges from Hawaii to coast of Africa and Red Sea, and also in eastern tropical Pacific. About 9 inches in length. The body is striped with bands of black, white and yellow, with smaller bands of red and blue. The shape of the body is unique, unmistakable and almost a world-wide symbol of the coral reef environment.

MORAY EELS
Muraenidae

WAVEY-LINED MORAY
Gymnothorax undulatus

Ranges from Hawaii to the coast of Africa. Can reach a length of 36 inches. A dark body with an irregular pattern of white lines.

MOTTLED MORAY
Gymnothorax eurostus

Found in Hawaiian waters, perhaps the most common moray. Up to 24 inches in length. Color of body varies from gray to brown or black, with light spots. Difficult to distinguish from several other moray eels.

ZEBRA MORAY
Echidna zebra

Ranges from Hawaii to the coast of Africa and is also found along the western American coast. Can reach 30 inches in length. Easily identified because of its distinctive body pattern. Body is dark brown or black, with many yellow bands or lines encircling the body.

DRAGON MORAY
Muraena pardalis

Ranges from Hawaii to Mauritius. May reach 36 inches in length. Thought to be the most intelligent of Hawaiian fishes, and also has the most vivid coloration. Covered with spots of many different colors, and has a curved jaw full of prominent teeth.

PARROTFISHES
Scaridae

RED-LIPPED PARROTFISH
Scarus rubroviolaceus

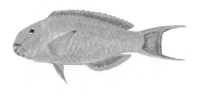

Ranges from Hawaii to the Indian Ocean, and also in the eastern tropical Pacific. Can reach 28 inches in length. The colors of this fish, like so many other parrotfishes, are difficult to describe. All parrotfishes have a number of different color phases, related both to maturity and to the change of sex. Males are orange on the upper part of the body and green on the lower part. Females are a more uniform brownish red.

UHU
Scarus perspicillatus

Known only from Hawaiian waters. Can be 24 inches long. Males have mottled but brilliant green and blue colors. Females are reddish brown.

SORDID PARROTFISH
Scarus sordidus

Ranges from Hawaii to the Indian Ocean, the coast of Africa, and the Red Sea. Can reach 40 inches in length. A common species in Hawaii, with the usual color changes occurring during growth. Adult males are green.

PUFFERS AND PORCUPINEFISHES
Tetraodontidae and Diodontidae

SPINY BALLOONFISH
Arothron hispidus

Ranges from Hawaii to coast of Africa. Generally about 12 inches in length. Body is grayish brown, back has white spots and belly has many dark lines. Entire body is covered with small spines.

CROWNED SHARP-NOSED PUFFERFISH
Canthigaster cinctus

Ranges from Hawaii to the coast of Africa and the Red Sea. Up to 5 inches in length. Body is black and white, and fish is most easily identified by its many orange spots and by its long sloping snout.

WHITE-SPOTTED SHARP-NOSED PUFFERFISH
Canthigaster jactator

Found in Hawaiian waters only. About 2 inches in length. Most easily identified by its prominent white spots and long pointed snout.

BALLOONFISH
Diodon holocanthus

This fish is found in all of the world's tropical oceans. About 12 inches in length. Brown and white body which is easily identified by prominent spines and brown band connnecting across the top of the head.

PORCUPINEFISH
Diodon hystrix

Also found throughout the world in tropical waters. A sizable fish, sometimes approaching 36 inches in length. Can be distinguished by its size, large eyes and very large head in comparison to the rest of the body.

RAYS
Mobulidae and Myliobatidae

MANTA RAY
Manta alfredi

This species of manta ray ranges from Hawaii to Polynesia. Up to 12 feet in width. Top of the body is dark gray, while the lower surface is white with a number of black blotches. Two horn-like fins project forward from the head on each side of the mouth. Very easily identified by its unique body shape.

SPOTTED EAGLE RAY
Aetobatus narinari

Found in all tropical waters in the Atlantic, Pacific and Indian Oceans. Up to 7 feet in width. Upper body is dark, covered with white spots. Has a prominent snout, but does not have the horns found in manta rays.

SCORPIONFISHES
Scorpaenidae

HAWAIIAN LIONFISH
Pterois sphex

This species is found only in Hawaiian waters. May reach 10 inches in length. Body is reddish brown with white vertical lines. This fish is easily identified by its prominent spines on the dorsal and pectoral fins, all of which are venomous.

UGLY-FACED SCORPIONFISH
Scorpaenopsis cacopsis

Found in Hawaii only. A large scorpionfish, reaching 20 inches. The body includes mottled colors of red, brown, white, yellow and black and is extremely well camouflaged. A truly ugly fish that is easy to identify, once it can be distinguished from its surroundings.

SHARKS
Carcharhinidae

SANDBAR SHARK
Carcharhinus milberti

Found around the world in the warm portions of the Atlantic, Pacific and Indian Oceans. The most common shark in Hawaii but very timid. May reach 6 feet in length. The top of the body is gray or brown, while the belly is white. Most easily identified by its large dorsal fin which is close to the head.

WHITE-TIPPED REEF SHARK
Triaenodon obesus

Found throughout all of the warmer portions of the Pacific Ocean. Can be up to 7 feet in length. Identified by a white spot on its dorsal fin. One of the few Hawaiian sharks that does not have to keep moving to breathe.

SQUIRRELFISHES
Holocentridae

BIGEYE SQUIRRELFISH
Myripristis amaenus

Ranges throughout the western and central Pacific Ocean. Can reach 14 inches in length. Body is pink or red, and a purple bar extends upward from the eye.

CROWN-FINNED SQUIRRELFISH
Adioryx diadema

Ranges from Hawaii to Africa and the Red Sea. Can reach 9 inches in length. Color of the body is variable, from deep red to light red. Most easily identified by about 9 white stripes on the body and a white throat.

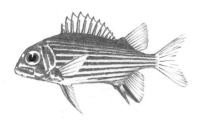

STRIPED SQUIRRELFISH
Adioryx xantherythrus

Known only from Hawaii. Up to 7 inches long. Another fish with a red body and 9 or 10 white lines on the sides, with a bright white belly. The most common squirrelfish in Hawaii.

SURGEONFISHES
Acanthuridae

ACHILLES TANG
Acanthurus achilles

Ranges from Hawaii to Micronesia. Can reach a length of 10 inches. Prefers surge areas in shallow waters. Body is dark brown, and marked with a large red spot near the tail.

MUSTARD SURGEON
Acanthurus guttatus

Ranges from Hawaii to the Indian Ocean. Generally 6 to 8 inches in length. Another fish that prefers surge areas in shallow waters. Body is brownish, and marked with 3 or 4 vertical bands.

WHITE-BANDED SURGEON
Acanthurus leucopareius
Ranges from Hawaii to Micronesia. From 6 to 8 inches in length. Body is brownish, and is most easily identified by white band, fringed with brown, near eye.

LAVENDER TANG
Acanthurus nigrofuscus
Ranges from Hawaii to coast of Africa and Red Sea. A small surgeonfish, up to 5 to 6 inches in length. Very common and aggressive. Body appears uniformally brown except in bright light which brings to life its lavender tinge.

RED-SHOULDER TANG
Acanthurus olivaceus
Ranges from Hawaii to the East Indies. To 12 inches in length. Body is grayish brown. Fish is easily identified by large horizontal orange band just behind the head.

MANINI
Acanthurus sandvicensis
Range is limited to Hawaii. Generally about 6 or 7 inches in length. Body is light gray and marked with 6 very distinct black vertical bars. Taxonomists consider the manini to be a subspecies of *Acanthurus triostegus*, found from the Eastern Pacific to the Indian Ocean.

PURPLE SURGEON
Acanthurus xanthopterus
Ranges throughout tropical waters of Pacific and Indian oceans, and off western Mexico to east Africa. A very large surgeon, sometimes 24 inches in length. Body is gray with yellow fins marked with blue and brown bands.

PALANI
Acanthurus dussumieri
Ranges from Hawaii to the coast of Africa. Another large surgeon, up to 16 inches in length. Body is pale brown, but most distinctive marking is tail fin, which is bright blue.

KOLE
Ctenochaetus strigosus
Ranges from Hawaii to the Indian Ocean and the coast of Africa. A small surgeon, not more than 7 inches in length. Very abundant, especially in shallow water. Body is brown, and the fish is most easily identified by a bright yellow ring around the eye.

YELLOW TANG
Zebrasoma flavescens
Ranges from Hawaii to the Indian Ocean. Up to 8 inches in length. The fish is easily identified by its brilliant yellow body.

SAILFIN TANG
Zebrasoma veliferum

Ranges from Hawaii to possibly the coast of Africa. Up to 16 inches long. Easy to identify when its very large dorsal and anal fins are erected. Otherwise, look for large vertical bars on a bright yellow body.

UNICORN SURGEON
Naso unicornis

Ranges from Hawaii to the coast of Africa and the Red Sea. A large surgeon, which can reach 20 inches in length. Body is grayish brown, and the fish is identified by the horn on its head.

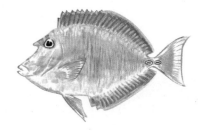

SHORT-HORNED UNICORN TANG
Naso brevirostris

Ranges from Hawaii to the coast of Africa. Up to 18 inches long. The body is grayish green, but the horn can be remarkably long, in spite of the fish's misleading name.

NASO TANG
Naso lituratus

Ranges from Hawaii to the coast of Africa and the Red Sea. Approximately 15 inches in length. Although the body is a plain dark brown, it is brilliantly marked with orange, yellow, blue and white. Easily identified by the bright orange spots surrounding the spines on each side of the tail.

TRIGGERFISHES
Balistidae
BLACK TRIGGERFISH
Melichthys niger

Ranges throughout tropical oceans. Can reach 14 inches in length. Although the body is virtually black, it has light blue stripes along the bases of the dorsal and anal fins, and has a striking appearance.

PINKTAIL TRIGGERFISH
Melichthys vidua

Ranges from Hawaii to the coast of Africa. Up to 15 inches long. Body looks like the black triggerfish, but dorsal, anal and caudal fins may be pink or white. Another fish with a distinctive appearance.

LAGOON HUMU
Rhinecanthus aculeatus

Ranges from Hawaii to the coast of Africa and the Red Sea. Reaches 9 inches in length. Has bold colors in patterns of gray, brown, blue, yellow and white which defy description.

PICASSO TRIGGERFISH
Rhinecanthus rectangulus

Ranges from Hawaii to the coast of Africa and the Red Sea. About 8 inches in length. Is strongly patterned with yellow, white and black.

WHITELINE TRIGGERFISH
Sufflamen bursa

Ranges from Hawaii to the coast of Africa and the Red Sea. About 7 inches in length. Delicately colored with browns, grays, and blacks. Most easily identified by 2 large black stripes behind the eye.

CHECKERBOARD TRIGGERFISH
Xanthichthys mento

Ranges from Hawaii eastward across the Pacific Ocean to tropical America. About 8 inches in length. Brightly colored red and orange fins on a brown body. Identified by 5 horizontal lines around the side of the head.

TRUMPETFISHES AND CORNETFISHES
Aulostomidae and Fistulariidae
TRUMPETFISH
Aulostomus chinensis

Ranges from Hawaii to the coast of Africa. Up to 24 inches in length. Most easily identified by its body shape. Has many variations in color and patterns, including green, brown and orange bodies and various variations of stripes, bands and spots.

CORNETFISH
Fistularia petimba

Ranges throughout the tropical oceans. Can reach 60 inches in length. More slender than the trumpetfish, with a long filament extending from the tail. Has a greenish body.

WRASSES
Labridae

SADDLEBACK WRASSE
Thalassoma duperreyi

Known only from Hawaii. Can be 12 inches long. Body is green and prominently marked by a wide orangish band around the body behind the head.

YELLOW-TAIL WRASSE
Coris gaimardi

Ranges from Hawaii to the coast of Africa and the Red Sea. Up to 15 inches in length. Adults are reddish with bright blue spots and a brilliant yellow tail. The juveniles of this fish have a completely different coloration with a dark red body and 5 prominent white patches.

BLACK-BANDED WRASSE
Coris flavovittata

This is a large wrasse, which can reach a length of 18 inches. It has a white body and is easily identified by bold black stripes along the upper part of the body. It also has 4 strong and protruding teeth.

PACIFIC HOGFISH
Bodianus bilunulatus

Ranges from Hawaii across the Indian Ocean. Another sizable wrasse, reaching a length of 24 inches. A light body, most easily identified by the black spots appearing at the base of the dorsal fin.

ORNATE WRASSE
Halichoeres ornatissimus

Ranges from Hawaii to Polynesia. Up to 7 inches long. Intricate color patterns of red, green, blue and black.

GRAY WRASSE
Thalassoma ballieui

Ranges from Hawaii to Polynesia. May reach 24 inches in length. Body is grayish marked by short vertical brown stripes.

PEARLSCALE RAZORFISH
Hemipteronotus niveilatus

Found only in Hawaii. To 10 inches long. Most easily identified by its body shape and its prominent forehead. Grayish body marked with yellow, orange, red, blue and white.

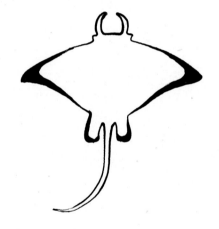

Bibliography

There are a number of excellent books on Hawaiian fishes, although most of them are scholarly in nature, and very few of them deal with behavioral questions. At the present time information on the behavior of coral reef fishes can, as a general matter, be found only in scientific articles. We have thus listed both the books and articles which contributed significantly to the preparation of this book.

Books

Fowler, H. W. 1928. *The Fishes of Oceania*. Volume X. Honolulu: Bishop Museum.

Goodson, G. 1973. *Fishes of Hawaii*. Palos Verdes Estates, California: Marquest Colorguide Books.

Gosline, W. A. & Brock, V. E. 1960. *Handbook of Hawaiian Fishes*. Honolulu: The University Press of Hawaii.

Hobson, E. S. & Chave, E. H. 1972. *Hawaiian Reef Animals*. Honolulu: The University Press of Hawaii.

Jones, O. A. & Endean, R. (Eds). 1973. *Biology and Geology of Coral Reefs*. Academic Press.

Jordan, D. S. & Evermann, B. W. 1905. *The Shore Fishes of the Hawaiian Islands*. Bulletin of the U.S. Fish Commission.

Kay, A. E. (Ed). 1972. *A Natural History of the Hawaiian Islands.* Honolulu: The University Press of Hawaii.

Lorenz, K. 1963. *On Aggression.* New York: Bantam Books, Inc.

Reese, E. S., Lighter, F. J. (Eds). 1978. *Contrasts In Behavior.* New York: John Wiley & Sons, Inc.

Roessler, C. 1978. *The Underwater Wilderness.* New York: Chanticleer Press, Inc.

Tinker, S. W. 1978. *Fishes of Hawaii.* Honolulu: Hawaiian Service, Inc.

Titcomb, M. 1972. *Native Use of Fish in Hawaii.* Honolulu: The University Press of Hawaii.

Articles

Barlow, G. W. 1974. Contrasts in social behavior between Central American cichlid fishes and coral-reef surgeon fishes. *American Zoologist.* 14: 9-34.

Davis, W. P. and Birdsong, R. S. 1973. Coral reef fishes which forge in the water column. *Helgolander Weissenschaftliche Meeresuntersuchungen.* 24: 292-306.

Ehrlich, P. R. 1975. The population biology of coral reef fishes. *Annual Review of Ecology and Systematics.* 6: 211-247.

Ehrlich, P. R. et al 1977. The behavior of chaetodontid fishes with special reference to Lorenz's "poster coloration" hypothesis. *Journal of Zoology (London).* 183: 213-228.

Fricke, H. W. 1973. Behavior as part of ecological adaption. *Helgolander Weissenschaftliche Meeresuntersuchungen.* 24: 120-144.

Hobson, E. S. 1972. Activity of Hawaiian reef fishes during the evening and morning transitions between daylight and darkness. *Fisheries Bulletin.* 70: 715-40.

Hobson, E. S. 1974. Feeding relationships of teleostean fishes on coral reefs in Kona, Hawaii. *Fisheries Bulletin.* 72: 915-1031.

Lobel, P. S. 1978. Diel, lunar, and seasonal periodicity in the reproductive behavior of the pomacanthid fish, *Centropyge potteri*, and some other reef fishes in Hawaii. *Pacific Science.* 32: 193-205.

Losey, G. S. 1971. Communication between fishes in cleaning symbiosis. In *Aspects of the Biology of Symbiosis*, Ed. T. C. Cheng, 45-76. Baltimore: Univ. Park Press.

Losey, G. S. 1972. The ecological importance of cleaning symbiosis. *Copeia 1972*: 820-33.

Myrberg, A. A. and Thresher, R. E. 1974. Interspecific aggression and its relevance to the concept of territoriality in reef fishes. *American Zoologist.* 14: 81-96.

Randall, J. E. 1961. A contribution to the biology of the convict surgeon fish of the Hawaiian Islands, *Acanthurus triostegus sandvicensis. Pacific Science.* 15: 215-72.

Randall, J. E. 1965. Grazing effect on seagrasses by herbivorous reef fishes in the West Indies. *Ecology.* 46: 255-60.

Randall, J. E. and Kanayama, R. K. 1972. Hawaiian fish immigrants. *Sea Frontiers.* 18: 144-53.

Randall, J. E. and Randall, H. A. 1960. Examples of mimicry and protective resemblance in tropical marine fishes. *Bulletin of Marine Science of the Gulf and Caribbean.* 10: 444-80.

Reed, S. A. 1978. Environmental stresses on the Hawaiian coral reefs. University of Hawaii. *Sea Grant College Program 1978.* 49-57.

Reese, E. S. 1964. Ethology and marine zoology. *Oceanography and Marine Biology: An Annual Review*, 1964. 455-88.

Reese, E. S. 1973. A comparative field study of the social behavior and related ecology of reef fishes of the family *Chaetodontidae.* Zeitschrift Fuer Tierpsvchologie. 37: 37-61.

Robertston, D. R., Sweatman, H. P. A., Fletcher, E.A. and Cleland, M. G. 1976. Schooling as a mechanism for circumventing the territoriality of competitors. *Ecology.* 57: 1208-1220.

Robertson, D. R. and Warner, R. R. 1978. Sexual patterns in the labroid fishes of the western Caribbean, II: the parrot-fishes (Scaridae). *Smithsonian Contributions to Zoology.* 255: 1-26.

Sale, P. F. 1977. Maintenance of high diversity in coral reef fish communities. *The American Naturalist.* 111: 337-359.

Smith, C. L. and Tyler, J. C. 1972. Space resource sharing in a coral reef fish community. *Results of the Tektite Program: Ecology of Coral Reef Fishes, Bulletin of the Natural History Museum of Los Angeles County.* 14: 125-70.

Warner, R. R. and Robertson, D. R. 1978. Sexual patterns in the labroid fishes of the western Caribbean, I: the wrasses (Labridae) *Smithsonian Contributions to Zoology.* 254: 1-27.

Index

In their professional lives Russell and Blyth Carpenter are respectively an attorney and a teacher. They are also active naturalists and share a determination to bring the often fascinating research of life scientists to less specialized readers. They are the founders of Natural World Press and live in Hillsborough, California, where they are raising three children.